Dillie the Deer

A True Story of Love, Healing, and Family

MELANIE R. BUTERA

with Diane Reverand

Regan Arts.

New York

Regan Arts.

65 Bleecker Street
New York, NY 10012

First Regan Arts hardcover edition, October 2015

Library of Congress Control Number: 2015946435

ISBN 978-1-94287210-8

Interior design by Nancy Singer
Cover design by Catherine Casalino
Front cover and title page photograph © Life on White / Alamy
Back cover photograph by Karen L. Clark

Printed in the United States of America

10 9 8 7 6 5 4 3 2 1

To my parents, Sal and Connie Butera

Thank you for your love and encouragement,
and for giving me the tools I needed
to live my dreams.

To my husband, Steve

Thank you for taking this journey with me
with so much love, wonder, and humor.

Disclaimers

This story is completely true, but events are related as I remember them.

I promised the wildlife department that I would make it clear that Dillie's circumstances are unique. Dillie was born on a farm, and her disposition and partial blindness have allowed her to be a well-acclimated pet in our household. I would never, and I do mean never, recommend anyone's having a deer as a house pet.

Please remember that in most states, including Ohio, it is illegal to take any animal out of the wild and make it a pet. It is illegal to allow domestic deer like Dillie and wild deer to have contact with each other. Although deer farming in Ohio is a fast-growing rural business, the federal and state regulations are very stringent and apply to our herd of one.

Dillie is fully permitted and registered with the state, and we comply with all the laws.

A portion of the proceeds from the sale of this book is donated to Dillie's charity for UNICEF and local animal rescue charities. You may donate directly to Dillie Dollars for Kids at:

www.razoo.com/story/Dillie-Dollars-For-Kids

Cont[ents]

CONTENTS

Introduction

I AM AN ANIMAL PERSON

My name is Melanie Butera, and I am an animal person. We animal people cherish our animals as our children. We care more about our pets than our sofas and carpets. We prepare meals for them, groom them, transform our homes for them, and shower them with affection. We treat them like royalty, serving them out of love. In return, our pets make us smile and laugh and give us companionship and protection.

When we look at an animal, whether a house cat, a goldfish, a Siberian tiger, or a parrot, we see beyond the fur, fins, and feathers to the beauty of creation. We experience the meaning of life, with all its wonder and mystery, hardship and joy. We recognize the presence of the Divine.

I connected with animals from the time I could toddle

over and hug Napoleon, our black and gray standard poodle, a gentle giant who would allow five hyperactive children to tug on his ears and ride him like a pony. He watched over all of us—we were his children. He was my bud throughout my childhood and adolescence. When I was lonely and sad, as I often was in those teenage days, Napoleon was my source of solace and strength. He passed away when I was seventeen and had just started college. He, too, was seventeen—we had been together our entire lives. Four decades later, Napoleon remains as great an influence on my life as any teacher or mentor I ever had.

During my childhood, I was naturally drawn to animals. I was always bringing home orphaned bunnies, baby birds, squirrels, kittens, puppies, opossums, and any other animal that needed a hand, which annoyed my busy mother to no end.

When I was in third grade, I found a brochure in class entitled "I Want to Be a Veterinarian." I knew immediately that this was my calling. I took the brochure home and read it aloud to Napoleon, stumbling over the names of the courses I would have to take: parasitology, immunology, endocrinology, and helminthology. I stayed awake all night looking up each word in the family encyclopedia. As I fell asleep, with Napoleon at my feet, I had an unusual clarity about what my life would be. Even though I had not yet taken a single class of veterinary medicine, nor survived any of the many, many all-night study sessions or grueling summer days in the equine rotation, nor diagnosed a single cat with lymphoma, or saved one dog with a ruptured bowel, I became a veterinarian that night.

When I was a teenager, Dean Le Beau, who was fresh out of school, was our family vet. After my mother told him of my aspirations, he ushered me back to a microscope and showed me a live heartworm larva squirming among a patient's red blood cells. He soon became my mentor. I volunteered at the Stark County Veterinary Clinic, where Dean served on the board.

Though it would take me another sixteen years, a great deal of sacrifice, and unwavering dedication to achieve my goal, I finally earned the right to put "DVM" after my name. Not long after I graduated from veterinary school, Dean hired me to work at the emergency clinic I later owned. In the two and a half decades that have passed since that proud graduation day at Ohio State, I have never stopped celebrating my good fortune. Of course, there have been difficult times. There have been mornings when I was so exhausted after working seventy straight hours that I literally crawled up the stairs to bed. There has been heartbreak when I could not save my patient or when the client would not even allow me to try. Yet I know my life could not have gone in any other direction. Becoming a vet was not a choice. This profession is not what I do; it is who I am.

My husband, Steve, is a grizzly bear of a man with a heart as big as nature. When we first met, people said it would never last because we were in many ways—okay, nearly all ways—complete opposites. I am cerebral, he is kinetic; I use logic, he's all about muscle and brawn; I am a technology geek, he is a Luddite; I come from a huge, loud Sicilian clan and he from a small, reserved family; I am a teetotaler, his middle name should be Coors Light. What is important is that we are both animal people. Steve and I have a deep respect for all creatures and see in them the spark of God. Animals are not only our livelihood but also our passion and purpose.

We settled in Northeast Ohio, where I grew up. For most of our marriage, our family business has been the local veterinary emergency clinic. The great physical and personal demands of emergency work took their toll on me. As I aged, it wasn't as easy to go days and days without sleep as it had been when I was twenty-eight. By necessity, in 2005, I sold the emergency clinic and eventually started a smaller general practice right down the street from our home.

Though Steve has never had the "joy" of sitting through that class in helminthology, the study of worms, he is naturally gifted with animals. I have witnessed injured hummingbirds perch on his workman's hands as he fed them nectar drop by drop. Animals seem to bond with him almost immediately. It amazes me. Even the wildest animals we work on are soothed by his touch. I have seen an injured hawk, who would not let anyone near him, hop onto Steve's extended forearm. A hissing, feral kitten could not resist him for long and soon snuggled against his big chest. He has that legendary Dr. Doolittle magic.

Throughout our years together, many, many animals have been in our lives. Some have been cherished children who will stay in our hearts forever. On the day we opened the clinic, we found Sally, our cat who lived to be twenty, left on the doorstep before we had even unlocked the door. Our first dog as a couple was a basset hound named Oh-Five. At the same time, we had a pet raccoon named Mary Margaret Beauregard Butler, who had been rescued from an abusive situation at five weeks. Miss Butts or Butts, as we called her, and Oh-Five were great pals, which surprised us, because hounds and racoons are natural enemies. She used to ride on Oh-Five's back when we walked in the park. She was a rascal who stole food from the microwave. On the day that Oh-Five died, she grieved for him, crying with the oddest, heartbreaking sound. And soon you will meet Dillie, Neffie, Lady, Spazz, Screamie, and Willie. We have had so many treasured pets, and I could write a book about each of them. Many have been temporary guests or patients who etched a smile on our hearts. Thousands have been wild animals who were with us only as they convalesced before returning to the wild. Whether these animal visitors had human caretakers or were creatures of God, each one brought us joy and love.

None of these animals ever moved into our hearts and completely took over until the summer of 2004. Love comes in the door in many ways. Sometimes it thunders in with the dopey gallop of an irrepressible Labrador retriever. Or it may tiptoe in on the lithe feet of a Siamese cat. It might even stride in with the beauty and elegance of a big red Thoroughbred. Love came into our life quite unexpectedly late one crisp June evening on the tiny hooves of a dying fawn.

We could not have known then that this struggling, blind creature would become so important to us. At the time, we didn't even believe she was going to survive the night. Yet, she was destined to find a place in our hearts and home forever.

The animals in our life have always returned the love we give them, with interest. This tiny, gasping fawn would return the love that saved her 10,000 percent, compounded daily. Her love bank was so plentiful that she would touch the hearts of people all over the world.

This dying fawn, rejected by her mother and unwanted by anyone in the world, became Dillie the Deer, love on hooves.

Chapter 1

~~~~~~~~

CONGRATULATIONS, IT'S A GIRL

The spring crop in the flower beds may be tulips and daffodils, but in veterinary emergency clinics, the spring crop is "T & D"—Trauma and Drama. Winters in Ohio are long, cold, wet, and oh, so gray. Pets crave good weather, just like their human parents. Spring brings out the puppy in every dog and the kitten in every cat.

In 2004, at the Stark County Veterinary Emergency Clinic, in Canton, Ohio, spring was in full bloom. Steve had just dropped me off for the night shift. Since I worked through the night on a high-pressure shift, Steve took me to work and picked me up in the morning. He did not like me to drive home exhausted. When I walked into the clinic, the waiting room was packed, and the phone was ringing incessantly.

"Your dog swallowed your girlfriend's underwear? Yes, you need to come in." Pat, our receptionist, deftly screened the calls, identifying the real emergencies. The other line rang again before she had even put the phone down.

"Stark County Emergency Clinic. How can we help you?" After a pause, she asked, "Did your dog eat the container along with your birth control pills or just the pills? Okay, good. Birth control pills are harmless as long as the dog isn't pregnant."

"Great!" Pat nodded as she listened to the caller's response. "Since your dog is a male, there shouldn't be a problem. There's no need to bring Rex in." A puzzled expression crossed her face. "You don't have to worry—Rex won't grow breasts because he ate your birth control pills. Have a good day, I have another call coming in."

"Hello, Stark County Vet Emergency Clinic. How can we help you? Your dog went through a plate-glass window chasing a squirrel and has an eight-inch piece of glass sticking out of his chest? Come on in!"

We were juggling case after critical case, desperately trying to keep all the balls in the air, without any patients crashing and dying. Angie triaged. She assessed the patients in the waiting room and decided who needed to be seen first. Critical patients would go right to the back, to our treatment area, which we considered the ICU. We had a surgery prep area, a surgery room, and a separate isolation area with glass walls so that we could see the patients even when we were not in the ward. Otherwise, the animals went to exam rooms and were seen in order of arrival. At my clinic, the exam rooms looked like miniature houses, each with a different architectural style, thanks to Steve's handiwork. Room one looked like a typical suburban home with gray aluminum siding and shutters. room two was a log cabin, and room three a Tudor cottage.

I did a physical on each ailing animal and discussed what needed to be done with clients, who were often overwrought. Sherry, Pat's daughter, was the most experienced assistant at the clinic. She coordinated treatment. She put in IVs and multitasked with Angie and Shawna to do the treatments.

Shawna and I had just finished working on an emotionally draining case in room three. We had lost a retired police dog from a ruptured splenic tumor. Shawna knew the K9 police officer. The dog's handler was weeping over the heroic German shepherd's lifeless body.

"He's no longer in pain now," I tried to comfort the heartbroken officer. Shawna stayed with him to console him. Then I went to work on a pit bull mix with a round steak bone trapped in his lower jaw.

It wasn't long before I heard the sound of many sirens from the parking lot. I left Sherry with the pit bull mix to see what the crisis was. When I looked out the window, I saw four police squad cars, sirens blaring and lights flashing. They had come to escort the deceased canine officer home. The police lined up at attention as the handler carried out his partner.

I put dogs to sleep every night at the clinic, but this was the only time I ever saw a police escort.

Pat came into the treatment area with a surprised expression and a blue-blanketed bundle in her arms and said, "You'll never believe what's here. . . ."

Pat had seen just about everything and was unflappable. Her agitation stopped me in my tracks.

"She's critical!" Pat announced. We all came running.

When Pat laid the bundle on the treatment table, a thin, long leg with a white hoof emerged. Pat unwrapped the tiny spotted creature, a dying fawn with a yellow ear tag nearly as big as her entire ear. The tag bore the number 60. Except for her long legs, she was no bigger than a young cat. I estimated that she weighed only about four pounds. Her eyes were a cloudy white from cataracts. Pieces of straw were stuck to her mouth, eyes, and nose.

We responded to the sight with an *"Awww,"* then snapped into our emergency routine. This baby needed the essentials: oxygen, warmth, fluids, and blood sugar.

"Where is she from?" I asked as I began clipping the neck of the motionless creature to gain access to the jugular vein.

"There's an Amish-looking man out there who resembles Santa," Pat said. "He says he's been here before."

I knew it had to be Al Glick, the deer farmer I had met at the clinic a few weeks earlier. Mr. Glick had tried to save the first buck born to his new prize buck, whose antlers were bigger than any other deer on his farm and for whom he'd paid nearly $20,000. Bucks from this sire could be worth just as much and could keep his farm running for years. The buck fawn was nearly dead as he loaded him into the truck and rushed off to my clinic. When they arrived an hour later, the baby had already passed away.

DOAs are sad, but when I'm working a very busy night at the ER, there's no time for me to process the sorrow. I have to move on to the next animal I can help. I often had to leave most of the grief counseling to my staff, who spent time with the clients and made paw prints, took hair clippings, and arranged for burial or cremation. I had spent some time with Mr. Glick the first night he came to the clinic.

Dressed in denim coveralls, Mr. Glick was hard of hearing, plain-spoken, and unassuming. He had been relieved to find out that I was willing to work on deer. I had collaborated with the wildlife department and rehabilitators for decades and had experience with fawns. My philosophy had always been that if the owner could get the animal to my door, it was my duty to try to help it.

That night, Mr. Glick had felt bad that the fawn had passed, but he hadn't been particularly attached to the baby. Eventually, our conversation moved on. We spoke about deer, goats, and other animals. I mentioned that Steve and I had a barn with horses and that we were thinking about adding some goats to our little farm.

Mr. Glick was a kind man, and I was glad he'd returned with the sick fawn for my help.

The fragile baby before me was breathing a little better with the oxygen mask on. Everything was ready to place the intravenous line, but I had to check with Mr. Glick before proceeding. When a child goes to a hospital, no one ever has to stop lifesaving treatment to check if the parents want to save the child, but this step is essential in veterinary medicine.

Pat rushed Mr. Glick into exam room three, the Tudor cottage.

"Hi, Mr. Glick," I said, as I entered the room. "This baby is very critical."

"I know," he responded, tugging his grizzled beard. "It's a miracle she's even alive. She's three days old and hasn't nursed at all."

"We need to get an intravenous line in her if we're going to save her. Do you want me to go ahead?"

"Well, Doc," he answered slowly, "here's the thing . . ."

My heart sank. I didn't want to euthanize this beautiful creature whose life had just begun.

"She's blind," the farmer continued. "She has real bad cataracts. I can't keep her on the farm. I wouldn't be able to breed her or sell her."

Mr. Glick told me the story of the tiny deer. The fawn was born a throwaway. She was a triplet, and her mother determined right away that she was not worth saving. The other two fawns were strong bucks who suckled greedily. A third the size of her brothers, she was too weak and small to survive.

Nature could be cruel, making mothers sacrifice a baby for the good of the herd. The doe knew instinctively that she had to save her energy and life-giving milk for the stronger boys. "Her mother pushed her aside," Mr. Glick said. "If another doe hadn't tried to care for her, she wouldn't be alive now."

His farm consisted of a small herd of fewer than thirty deer. Despite being captive-bred and farm-raised, his deer rarely lost their fear of humans. Every morning and night, when Mr. Glick entered the enclosure to feed and water the deer, the clang of the gate sent the herd leaping away to cower in the far corners of the fenced-in area. Sometimes, a few deer jumped against the ten-foot fencing, the racket further scaring the rest of the herd.

Only one doe welcomed Mr. Glick to the pen, usually trotting to greet him while the others bounded away. She'd lick his shoes and hands as he bent down to greet her. He had named this special doe Sweetie because of her friendly disposition. Sweetie was barren. Since she was unable to produce fawns, she made no practical contribution to the farm. Farmed deer are used for everything from the velvet that coats growing antlers to venison. Mr. Glick's business was to produce big bucks that he sold to other deer farms to increase the value of their stock. At seven years old, Sweetie was unlikely ever to be of economic value to the farm, but of all the deer in the herd, she was the only one Mr. Glick had connected with. He couldn't part with Sweetie.

Three nights after the fawn was born, the ringing sound of the gate set off the usual chain of events. A chorus of clings and clangs began, followed by the bleats of a good spring crop of fawns. Mr. Glick noticed that something was wrong. Sweetie wasn't at the gate waiting. She didn't come trotting to him.

He worried that she was sick or injured. In the dark, he couldn't see the enclosure and didn't want to wait until morning to find her dead. Fearing the worst, he retrieved a kerosene lamp and blanket, his wife following a few steps behind.

They found Sweetie lying on folded legs in the far cor-ner of the pen, as peaceful as could be, nestled against a newborn fawn. As Mr. Glick crouched down, Sweetie extended her neck and licked his nose in recognition, then licked the fawn next to her.

Al recognized the baby by her ear tag, number 60. He had seen her mother deliver her nearly three days earlier. He had tagged her as required, but never expected her to survive the day. He could see the clouds in her eyes and knew she was blind.

But Sweetie had her own plans. She claimed the fawn as her own. The warmth of her body kept the baby alive, but she had no milk for the fawn, who had not nursed since her birth and was losing strength. The newborn was dying.

Al knew the only way to save her now was to get her to a vet, even though a good farmer cannot invest thousands or even hundreds of dollars to save an animal, regardless of how much he or she might want to. Mr. Glick's farm was struggling. Deer farmers in Ohio could no longer sell their deer to farms in other states because of a chronic wasting disease, which is much like mad cow disease. The new law had reduced Mr. Glick's income significantly. He couldn't afford a vet bill for a blind fawn.

I prepared myself for him to say, "Just put her to sleep."

When he said, "I thought maybe you might want her if you can save her," I was caught off guard.

"Pardon me?"

"Well, I know you said you had a barn and all, and you love deer, so if you want to try to save her you can. I just can't put any money into her, so you would be on your own."

"I'll try," I answered, not really thinking ahead. I didn't expect the fawn to survive the night.

"If you can get her to nurse, here's some goat's milk."

Mr. Glick placed a Mason jar full of milk from Gertie, his goat, on the exam table.

"We'll leave it in God's hands," I said. Then I got back to work.

My team sprang into action. I placed the intravenous catheter into the jugular vein of the baby deer, securing the catheter with sutures and a yellow smiley-face bandage wrapped gently around her neck. Sherry rinsed and lubricated the fawn's opaque eyes, wrapped her in a warming blanket, and gently placed her in an ancient baby incubator that had been discarded by a human hospital and painted lavender by Steve and his paint gun. Normal temperature for a fawn is 102 degrees. This one's temperature was not even registering on the thermometer, which reads as low as ninety-two degrees.

I wrote up the ICU treatment sheet, and Sherry, Shawna, and Angie took care of the fawn's evening treatments. After nearly two hours, the baby's condition began to improve ever so slowly. Fluids were flowing into her blood, delivering the essential electrolytes and sugar she needed to survive. Her breathing had become regular, and we could diminish the oxygen flow to the incubator.

Sherry took her temperature. "Ninety-four!" she announced, excited. "And look—she's shivering."

This was progress! Shivering was her body's natural response to help her warm up. It was a sign that the fawn was regaining consciousness.

I was working the night shift from six at night until eight in the morning; the lay staff changed at midnight when Rhonda and Tina arrived. A few minutes later, we had to rush into surgery with a Great Dane suffering from a twisted stomach. Pat and Sherry stayed past their shifts, volunteering their time to sit with the baby. Sherry tended to fawn number 60's medical needs, adjusting the IV fluid pump, massaging dextrose sugar into her gums, and checking vital signs. Pat sat and held the fawn in her arms all night, rocking her and talking to her as if she were holding her own grandchild.

Spazz, our clinic cat, put his front paws on Pat's thighs and checked on the bundle in her arms. He was a twenty-pound butterball of long, thick fur with yellow eyes, an unusually short tail, and claws he was quick to use to show the world he was in charge. Except for one little white spot in his mane, he was completely black. He had been brought in one night on emergency as a "good Sam, HBC," which means a kind animal lover, not his owner, had seen Spazz get hit by a car and brought him in for assistance. He had a concussion and a broken shoulder blade. The X-rays revealed that Spazz was already a survivor. At some point, someone had shot him with a .22, leaving a slug behind in his neck. He responded well to emergency treatment, but there was no one to pick him up and take him home.

The clinic crew grew to love this scruffy fur ball. He climbed up the cage bars to peer in at every patient. Watching a corpulent cat climb up a five-foot-tall cage bank rung by rung and peek in on the newest patients was a sight. Most of the animals greeted him with a bark or a hiss. He hissed back and ran away. This was just his way of saying, "This is my clinic. Now, get well and get out!"

Some of the patients were too sick to care that he was peering at them. He stuck in a furry paw and touched all of them to see if they were still alive. He was doing triage when he checked on Dillie.

By morning the fawn was attempting to stand on her wobbly, disproportionately long legs, but she would not nurse on her own and didn't seem to know what she was supposed to do. Most babies of any mammal species, including humans, will suckle instinctively when a nipple or finger is inserted in their mouths. Not this fawn. She had no suckle reflex and had to be fed Gertie's milk one drop at a time from a syringe.

That's what Rhonda and I were doing when Steve arrived to pick me up at eight a.m. When he came through the doors, he stopped in his tracks, took one look at 60, and instantly fell in love.

Through the years, Steve has helped me with thousands of animals that the clinic had rescued. He once carried around a basket of hungry robin fledglings that had to be fed hourly throughout a day of construction work. The same huge, coarsened hands that could wield a sledgehammer like a matchstick had also held an injured hummingbird that needed syringe-fed nectar.

Steve took the milk-filled syringe from Rhonda and continued the feeding, explaining his technique to my assistant of twenty years. "Just dribble a little milk on the tongue, and let her taste it. Then, when she swallows, give a little more."

Rhonda had watched Steve foster various creatures, from abandoned puppies to baby opossums, and knew not to come between him and his charges.

I told him how 60 had come to the clinic.

"I don't want to put her out in the barn right now. It's too cold." Steve was excited. "We can bed her down in the garage, then move her to the barn later. I'll get some lumber today and build a separate area for her away from the horses."

"Whoa," I said, "Slow down. She's not even out of the woods yet. Let's see if she survives."

"Survive? Of course she will," Steve insisted as the fawn suckled on his goat-milk-coated finger. "I am not going to let her die."

The fawn bleated softly and licked Steve's cheek.

"Congratulations, guys," Rhonda said with a laugh. "It's a girl!"

Chapter 2

~~~~~

And Baby Makes Seven

Steve and I made the short trip from the clinic to our home with our new child, 60. Swaddled in a soft, pink blanket, the fawn traveled on my lap as Steve drove. Though still weak, the infant was able to hold up her head and peer out the window, licking it curiously. Her neck was still wrapped in the smiley-face bandage to keep her jugular catheter secure. She would complete her convalescence at our house.

It was only a fifteen-minute trip from the city of Canton, where the emergency clinic was located, to our home in the village of Canal Fulton. Settled in the early 1800s, Canal Fulton had kept much of its vintage charm. Named for the Ohio and Erie Canals, where nearly a century ago mules had pulled canal boats through town, the village had barely changed. Downtown was three blocks long, on the edge of a canal dug by hand in 1827. The brick buildings were no greater than three stories. Though there was not a large Amish population in Canal Fulton, a horse and buggy would not look out of place clopping down the main street.

Nestled among thick woods of maple, oak, and flowering apple trees, our house sits on a hill on the outskirts of town, completely isolated from others in the summer. When the trees were bare, the neighborhood was just visible behind the back fence. The view from the front porch included a lake shimmering through the trees. As we brought the fawn up the drive, I noticed the woods had already blossomed enough to hide the world beyond the property. A red barn sat about one hundred feet from the house in a fenced corral. Steve and some of his friends had built the barn a few years earlier so that Catherine, an employee of mine who had worked for me since high school, could house her two horses while she attended veterinary school in Columbus.

As Steve's white Dodge pickup chugged up the hill, the horses trotted out of the barn to the edge of the fence to greet us, as they always did. Kibbles, an older Thoroughbred gelding, and Cammie, a young, feisty quarter horse mare, always whinnied until Steve came to see them at the fence. Usually, he rubbed their noses and slipped them a peppermint or two, but today he was on a mission. Steve waved to the horses as he got out of the truck and ran around to take the fawn from my lap.

"I will be out later, guys!" Steve shouted to them.

Disappointed, they sauntered back to the barn.

With the blind fawn in his arms, Steve opened the back

door of the house. Lady, our black standard poodle, who wore pink bows on her coifed ears, came running to greet us with one of her toys in her mouth, tail wagging wildly. When anyone arrived at our home, Lady always brought the visitor a gift. She searched the house for one of her toys. If she couldn't find a toy, she grabbed a shoe or any other item she could reach. Once she even grabbed a candlestick from the dining room table. On the day of the fawn's arrival, she chose a toy she had claimed for herself at Christmastime—a stuffed reindeer.

Our motley crew proceeded into the house. Steve laid the pink-blanketed bundle on the kitchen island and started warming some of the goat's milk for the next feeding. Lady poked her nose into the bundle and sniffed, and then she jumped up with her front paws against the edge of the island and met 60, nose-to-nose, for the first time. The little fawn responded to the warm poodle nose against hers with a loving lick. Lady growled and bolted into the dining room.

Some dogs are instinctively maternal and will nurture toys, orphaned rabbits, or other puppies. On the maternity scale, Lady rated a zero. As the dog of a veterinarian, especially one who does wildlife rehabilitation, Lady was accustomed to encountering critters that needed care. Puppies, kittens, fledgling birds, opossums, squirrels, potbellied piglets—just about any creature with fur or feathers—had been fostered in our house at one time. Lady hated them all.

She kept darting into the kitchen for another look at 60 and a quick sniff, then retreated each time with a grumble and a growl.

Our cat, Neffie, was perched high above the scene, on the cupboards over the refrigerator. Neffie, an Abyssinian, was named for Nefertiti, the queen of ancient Egypt, and she had the regal attitude of her namesake. From her lofty perch, she surveyed the activity below with indifference.

Our diverse family—two humans, a standard poodle, two horses, and an aloof cat—now had a seventh member, a baby fawn.

I set up the downstairs bathroom as a makeshift ICU. The fawn was still not nursing well and needed to get her fluids intravenously. I left Steve in charge, with the fawn bedded down in a laundry basket and the electric IV fluid pump hanging from the towel bar. The deer seemed to be doing so much better. I hoped she would continue to improve during the day. I only had about a six-hour window to sleep before heading back to the office, so I climbed the stairs to get some rest.

Steve went to the lumber store and started adding a partition to the barn so the fawn could live there and get away from the horses if she wanted to. Convinced he had the usual apple in his pocket, the horses were tugging at his jacket. Kibbles and Cammie kept pestering him while he hammered and fashioned the new stall. Kibbles tugged on his tool belt as he stood on the ladder, and Cammie, wicked girl that she was, laid her ears back flat and tried to bite him from behind. Each time, Kibbles scolded her with a bite of his own, and she finally retreated a few feet. Steve soon realized that this new stall alone would not be enough to keep the curious horses away from the fawn. He would have to fence off a portion of the corral for 60.

Kibbles came over and nuzzled him as he worked. The Thoroughbred's head towered over Steve's six-foot frame. Twenty years earlier, Kibbles had been a winning race-horse, and he retained the majesty of his breed. He was as gentle as he was tall and seemed very wise. Steve put his arm around Kibble's muscular, brown neck and patted him as they both surveyed the view from the barn. They had become best buddies in the short time Steve had cared for him.

Through the trees, the morning sun shimmered across the lake. The only sounds were the spring birds calling to each other in the woods and the crunch, crunch, crunch of Cammie chewing her grain.

"This is a good spot for her," Steve said to Kibbles.

Every half hour, he walked to the house to check on the patient. She wasn't doing as well as he had hoped, and he was worried. She would only take a few dribbles of milk at a time and still wouldn't nurse from the baby bottle. She was able to hold her head up and occasionally tried to stand, but she remained very weak. Then she took a drastic turn for the worse. She developed diarrhea, which could prove fatal to a fragile animal who weighed less than four pounds.

In the daylight, Steve could see the dense cataracts in both her eyes. She didn't even blink when he approached her with the syringe. Her blindness broke his heart.

When I came downstairs, he was sitting on the floor of the makeshift ICU with 60 wrapped in a blanket in his lap. "Poor little thing," he said as he dribbled the milk on the fawn's tiny tongue.

Since 60 hadn't rallied, Steve and I agreed that the baby

had to go back to the clinic with me that night. The goat's milk was not a substitute for her mother's milk. The colostrum— the natural antibodies that are passed from mother to baby during the first feeding—was essential for survival. This fawn had been deprived of that protection. We were doing all we could, but sometimes love and medicine are not enough.

"I don't think this milk is agreeing with her." I was worried that the goat's milk could be the cause of the diarrhea. "We better stop at the store on the way to the clinic to pick up some canned goat's milk."

Steve wanted to show me the work he had done on the barn, so we grabbed a couple of apples for the horses and walked out, with Lady leading the way. Both horses clopped lazily along the sidewalk inside their corral and greeted us at the fence. The horses crushed the apples with a single chomp, the juice squirting all over.

Steve showed me the entrance he had cut into the existing barn wall and pointed to where he was planning to build a fence so that the horses would leave 60 alone. His plan was to construct a stall with a separate entrance and a separate corral for her. He started talking about getting another deer or goat to keep her company.

I was feeling a bit less optimistic. "Let's not get ahead of ourselves. She's not ready to move out here yet anyway. We can talk about that when she's stronger."

That move never happened. The fawn saw to that herself.

Chapter 3

~~~~~~~

Universal Mother's Milk

Steve and I bundled up the fawn for a trip in the truck and another night at the emergency clinic. I got into the truck, and Steve handed me the tiny fawn, whom I cradled in my arms. On the way to the clinic, we stopped at our local drugstore to buy Meyenberg's canned goat's milk. Canned goat's milk seems to be a universal formula for many infant mammals, including humans, so you can usually find it near the infant formulas.

Steve hopped out of the truck and trotted inside. There must have been an epidemic of colicky babies that day, because the store was sold out of canned goat's milk. The fawn was going to have to stick with Gertie's milk for another night.

We arrived at the clinic about an hour before the opening

bell and found a client already there talking to Pat, who always came to work early since clients often arrived before the clinic was open.

I transferred the bundled fawn to Pat and followed a trail of blood to triage the early patient, a pit bull with a bleeding paw. We saw this type of injury often at the clinic. Pat had already bandaged the foot to curb the bleeding, a simple thing that many distraught pet owners fail to do. The young man who owned the dog was alarmed by how much blood his dog was losing and was worried that the dog would bleed out. He rushed him right to the clinic without taking the time to bandage his foot. He had placed the dog on a towel and was upset that the dog had bled all over his car. Common sense got lost in panic.

The underside of a dog's paw is extremely vascular. The tiniest nick in the web of blood vessels will produce copious bleeding. I sedated the pit bull and put a couple of sutures in a wound not much bigger than a pencil point to stop the bleeding.

While I was dealing with the pit bull, Pat, wearing her favorite *I Love Lucy* scrubs, wrapped 60 up in her arms and brought her to the back treatment area. "Maybe you should call her Lucy," she said to Steve.

"I don't know what we're going to call her yet," he answered. "I don't think Mel wants to give her a name until we see if she's going to live."

For me, a name meant commitment. Giving 60 a name meant we were bringing her into our hearts and home forever, but 60 was still not out of the woods. The greater our bond, the greater the loss would be if she didn't make it.

"Maybe giving her a name will help her live," Pat said.

Steve took the suggestion to heart. "You're right, Pat. She needs a name."

As the rest of the staff arrived for the night, Steve took off on a quest for canned goat's milk. Store after store either did not have it or had never heard of it. In desperation, he stopped at a local farm supply business and purchased powdered lamb milk replacer. I'd never had much success with it, but we needed to try something else, and fast.

Worried that the lamb milk replacer wouldn't work, Steve stopped at a grocery store to pick up supplies for a homemade mammal formula we'd used on orphaned raccoons and opossums:

1 cup evaporated cow's milk
1 cup water
1 egg yolk
1 tablespoon honey or Karo
1 dash of baby vitamins

He headed down the baking aisle in search of evaporated milk. As he reached for the familiar red-and-white can, his heart stopped. By error or perhaps divine intervention, there, covered in a blanket of dust, was a huge supply of an item that doesn't belong in the baking aisle: canned Meyenberg's goat milk, enough to feed the tiny fawn for a month. Steve scooped every last can into his cart and rushed back to the clinic.

Pat was sitting behind the large, hexagonal reception desk with 60 in her lap and the IV pole beside her chair. She was doing extra duty. The rest of the staff was in the middle of a C-section, busy resuscitating thirteen Newfoundland puppies

"I found the goat's milk!" Steve exclaimed, holding a can up like Excalibur.

Lady trotted in behind him, greeting Pat and growling at the strange creature in her lap. Steve prepared the formula. Right away, the baby began to nurse from the bottle for the first time. The transformation seemed miraculous. The fawn was sucking steadily and kicking out her long legs as she did. There were now fourteen babies a-nursing at the clinic—thirteen chubby black puppies and one tiny, spotted deer.

Suddenly, amid the chorus of crying puppies, there was a loud *baaaaa*. Sixty was waking up. I turned my head in surprise as the bleats continued.

"She's getting stronger!" Pat exclaimed.

For the first time since Mr. Glick had brought in the fawn, I felt confident that she would make it. I looked at Steve and saw the relief and joy on his face.

He put his hand on my shoulder and said, "Life is good."

Steve headed out to his truck with Lady trotting behind him. I watched him pause to look up at the clear, starry sky. I knew how happy he was and felt that same joy.

Chapter 4

A Bright Yellow Name

As Steve drove us home the next morning, I struggled to hold on to the fawn. She kicked, craned her neck, and pushed her head out the window. In the backseat of the cab, Lady was sucking a stuffed toy like a pacifier. Every time the fawn thrust one of her delicate legs toward the backseat, Lady growled a warning.

Kibbles and Cammie had heard the Cummins diesel engine before the truck started up the drive and were waiting for us at the fence. They nodded and whinnied, calling for Steve to bring them a treat.

I set the baby down inside the backyard fence and shook my arms, which ached from restraining the surprisingly strong, squirming fawn. Baby 60 did not seem a bit afraid and moved right to a flower bed. Very curious about the visitor, Lady repeatedly snuck up, sniffed her, and ran away.

"We need to give her a name," Steve said.

My grandmother Rose was fighting an illness at the time and was very much on our minds. "How about Rosie?" I suggested.

"No," Steve answered. "I don't think your granny would appreciate that. She's not much of an animal person."

Just then, the fawn slipped in the mulch and tumbled into a bright patch of blooming daffodils, bleating in dismay.

"Daffodil," Steve said.

Seeing the baby tangled amid the yellow flowers, we both knew instantly that the name was perfect. Steve righted the newly christened Daffodil, as lovely as the spring itself, and she licked Steve's hand. "Hi, Dillie," he said, giving her a nickname.

Then he picked her up and carried her into her home.

Chapter 5

Dean to the Rescue:

The Triumph of Experience

Dr. Dean LeBeau, my mentor, retired in 2002 at the age of fifty-five. He had been diagnosed with prostate cancer and wanted to spend more time enjoying life with his family. Fortunately, the surgery took care of his cancer. Even after he retired, though, he regularly stopped by to visit me at the clinic. He couldn't help himself. He asked questions about each of our cases. We had informal "rounds." He examined and talked to the patients. He offered priceless advice on how to treat the animals. He was always a teacher, always a mentor, and always, always a vet.

Dean stopped by one busy night while I was working on a Dalmatian who had been vomiting for several days.

A greenhorn doctor, who had just started working for me, asked me to ultrasound the patient to check for a foreign body. He didn't want the usual barium X-ray series, because he "didn't believe in barium series."

I complied, biting my tongue, because I had no idea a barium series was a religion that required belief. To avoid early conflict, I agreed to do an ultrasound instead.

Dean and I chatted, and as we did, he began performing a physical exam on the Dalmatian. He checked the gums and tested the skin for dehydration. He asked for my stethoscope and listened to the heart, lungs, and abdomen. He knelt on the floor next to the dog and felt the belly. Still kneeling, he looked up at me and said, "This dog's got a washrag in the pylorus, where the stomach joins the small intestine."

At first I thought he was joking, but he was serious.

The newly minted DVM sneered at Dean's diagnosis. He was destined for a very short stay at my clinic. He and his millennial classmates were addicted to technology that did not exist in Dean's school days. He couldn't fathom that Dean could out-diagnose him and a seventy-thousand-dollar ultrasound machine with just his hands, brain, and a lifetime of experience.

Later that night, I took the Dalmatian to surgery. The dog had a bowel obstruction. Lodged in its pylorus was a blue-and-white-striped, 100 percent cotton washrag.

Dean was always an inspiration to me. Years before Dillie came to live with us, an injured fawn was brought into my clinic. Her back leg had a compound fracture, and the bone stuck out through her skin. I knew Wildlife would tell me to put her down, but I couldn't bear the thought of killing the beautiful, innocent creature.

Just as I was drawing up the euthanasia solution, Dean appeared in the doorway. He was at the emergency clinic to attend a monthly veterinary academy meeting held in our conference room.

He stroked the fawn's face. "What a beauty."

I pulled back the blanket and showed him the devastated leg.

"That's a bad one," he said.

"I'm just getting ready to euthanize her," I told him, my voice cracking.

"No, don't," he said. "We can fix that. We can pin it. She'll be good as new. I will come in tomorrow and fix it." He touched her face, and the fawn laid her head in his gentle hand.

"Dean," I said, "one problem: The state won't allow it. We're not able to rehab injured wild fawns anymore."

He waved his hand.

"I don't work for the state," he said, simply. "I work for God."

The fawn recovered, and we released her back into the wild. She visited our house to eat the hay Steve left out from time to time, her life extended by Dean's grace.

Chapter 6

Instinct or Extinct

Dillie's first nursery was very humble. In the garage attached to the house, Steve had prepared a bed with some blankets and straw. He had made a mini-stall, about two feet high, with some wooden planks. Once placed in her cozy den, Dillie curled up and tucked her head between her spindly legs.

In the wild, deer moms leave their babies alone when they go off to feed. The babies know instinctively to hunker down and keep their heads low to avoid becoming a predator's blue plate special. Preyed-upon animals, like deer and rabbits, spend their entire lives in fear that they are going to be eaten by something: coyotes, cougars, foxes, hawks, dogs, cats, and, of course, people. These species developed finely tuned senses and instinctive behaviors to protect them. Eventually, Darwinism's harsh mathematics creates a population especially adept at doing one and only one thing: surviving.

Even though Dillie had never known a second in the wild, nor had ten generations of her farm-bred ancestors, she still displayed the basic survival instincts encoded into her DNA. Curling up in the fetal position and burying herself in the straw was a direct result of millennia of evolution. She had no reason to fear that a cougar was going to break into her home and maul her in the garage. She was just doing what her genes instructed, but her genes didn't tell her everything. With her vision impaired, she didn't seem to recognize her own species. She was attracted to the first warm, fuzzy body she encountered, and that body just happened to be a standard poodle.

Lady seemed especially concerned that she was not the object of everyone's attention. She watched every interaction Steve or I had with Dillie and would sometimes nudge us to be petted when we were tending to the fawn. Lady snuck up on Dillie and probed her with her moist nose. She sniffed her up and down.

Dillie felt Lady's nose on her, sensed her body heat, and knew exactly what to do. She jumped up and tried to nurse—from one horrified standard poodle. Lady yelped and growled, then backed away as fast as her legs could retreat. Dillie followed. The little deer, who weighed less than five pounds, was small enough to fit right under Lady's belly, and she kept searching for a place to suckle.

When Lady slunk away, Dillie chased her. The game of tag went on until Steve interrupted it with a bottle of freshly warmed goat's milk. As soon as Dillie tasted the drop of milk on her nose, she grabbed the nipple with her mouth and gulped the milk down.

"She certainly seems interested in nursing," he said, displaying the empty bottle.

"That was fast!" I laughed. "You'd better hold her over your shoulder now and burp her!"

Dillie took another three bottles just as greedily as the first and probably would have taken more.

"Don't give her too much right now," I advised. "Let her rest a little, and we can feed her again in a few hours."

Dillie curled up in her straw with a full belly and began to settle into her new life. She didn't know any other life existed. She didn't know about the wild fawns just an acre or so away from her whose lives would never be as easy or as carefree as hers. These fawns would struggle to avoid predators through their entire youth, struggle to survive through winters when food was scarce and they huddled against the cold, and struggle to outlast each hunting season. Dillie didn't even know about the lives of her own parent herd, including her protector Sweetie, who lived behind a chain-link fence until they were sold or butchered. Her life had started hard and she was blind, but she would never want for anything. She would never have a cold night or a hungry day. She would never know anything but safety, comfort, and love every day of her life.

Chapter 7

A Daily Parade

By the end of her first week in her new home, Dillie was strong, active, and gaining weight rapidly. Thanks to Mr. Meyenberg's magical milk, the nagging question was no longer "Will she survive?" but "How can we afford to feed a fawn who is drinking twenty dollars' worth of goat's milk a day?"

All vigor and curiosity, Dillie was a little spotted explorer, continually investigating the world around her despite her impaired vision. She probed her surroundings with her ears, nose, and tongue, listening, sniffing, and licking as she sampled grass, flowers, teddy bears, and soft blankets. Everything was a discovery.

From the very first day, she had imprinted on Steve as papa and protector. He gave her the bottles of goat's milk she craved. Afterward, he cradled her in his strong arms until she slipped off into a contented sleep.

Love shining in her clouded eyes, she followed Steve everywhere. She couldn't bear to be more than three steps away. If he walked too fast, she panicked, woefully bleating. He would stop in his tracks and call, "C'mon, Dillie, over here!" and she would rush to his side.

Dillie had learned to stop chasing Lady for milk. No longer pursued by a baby desperate to nurse, Lady had warmed up to Dillie and became her constant companion. She accompanied Dillie as she followed Steve around the yard. All three marched single file each morning around the swimming pool to the edge of the horse corral. Since I slept during the day, I would walk out on the front porch to check on them every couple of hours. Lady would always be right behind Steve. I watched with amusement as Dillie, distracted by a flower or a piece of clover, lagged behind and would have to catch up in a trot. I was amazed by her adventuresome nature. Other blind animals we had cared for were afraid of every little thing, even grass. Dillie was dauntless.

Their small parade always stopped at the corral. When Dillie heard the clip-clop of the horses as they wandered over to the fence to greet their visitors, she immediately applied the cervid antilock disc brakes and did not take another step. Although Dillie's vision was impaired, she was not completely blind and could discern large shapes and shadows. To Dillie, Kibbles and Cammie were huge and frightening.

Lady went right up to the fence. Kibbles leaned his

massive head over the rail to give her a big slurp on her back. Lady enjoyed the attention, wagging her tail as Kibbles gave her another sloppy horse kiss. Dillie kept her distance, no matter how much Lady wagged her tail. When she heard the horses' hooves clop and sensed their presence, she took off like a rocket, her tail fluffed and twitching.

If Dillie was going to move successfully to the barn, she had to adjust to her future roommates. Steve believed that if he exposed her to them every day, she wouldn't be traumatized when she finally joined the horses. He picked her up, cradling her in his arms, and she licked his face and beard. Even in the absolute security of Steve's embrace, she was still terrified of the seven-foot-tall equine shadow.

"C'mon, Dillie," he said softly to her. "They won't hurt you."

Every time Steve approached the fence with Dillie, she panicked and flailed her long legs out until he could no longer contain her. He would set her on the ground, and she would gallop, panting, to her safety zone ten feet away.

"Sorry, Kib," Steve said, patting the old boy between his ears. "Guess you don't get to meet your new friend today. Maybe tomorrow."

Steve, Lady, and Dillie continued their march around the yard, soaking up the sights, sounds, and smells of spring. The daffodils, forsythia, and tulips were all in full bloom, and the yard was vibrant with yellows and reds. The birds sang their praise of the season. The squirrels high in the trees chattered as the trio approached. The wonderful scent of spring was everywhere, a mixture of newly mown grass and hyacinth warmed by the sun.

Lady went from tree trunk to tree trunk, sniffing up and down for evidence of recent squirrel activity. She was an avid squirrel hunter, but could never catch one. She enjoyed tracking them to their trees and listening to them scold her from high above. After a while, she replied with a loud bark.

The bark frightened Dillie, who was on the grass exploring the different bushes in the yard. She ran toward Steve, who was leaning against a blooming crabapple tree.

"It's okay, girl," he said, scooping her up. "First those scary horses and now a bark. The world is a big place, isn't it? You have a lot to learn, little girl."

As I watched Steve comforting Dillie from my stakeout on the front porch, I fell in love with him all over again.

Chapter 8

An Odd Matched Set

During her first week with us, Dillie had been too weak to do much more than sleep. Most fawns can walk at birth and forage when they are only a few days old. Once Dillie started doing it, she followed Steve outside tirelessly. After she trooped around the yard with Steve and Lady that beautiful day, she returned to her straw-filled nursery in the garage, curled up, and promptly passed out.

Steve and I went into the house for a snack. When Dillie woke up alone in her bed in the garage, we were alarmed by her high-pitched squeaks. We looked to see what was wrong, but Dillie was fine. When we came closer, she licked our hands and faces and quieted down. When we left, she started bleating all over again. She made the same high-pitched noise wild fawns do when they're separated from their mothers for too long, like a baby crying for food. She wanted to be with the rest of us at all times.

Our smallest family member, Neffie, avoided Dillie the entire first week she was with us. But in the end, curiosity got the best of her. She could not resist investigating the strange noises coming from the garage. At first, she was not able to make sense of the creature she discovered. She crept forward, until her nose was nearly at the stranger's shoulder. Dillie sensed Neffie there, turned her head, and licked. Neffie nearly jumped out of her skin. She hissed and beat a fast retreat.

During Dillie's first week with us, the tiny, dignified cat repeatedly visited the fawn, getting a little bolder each time. She discovered that the odd creature was not going to hurt her. There was a bonus in the nesting area—she could curl up on soft blankets right next to a four-legged heater. It was cat heaven. She began to nestle in next to Dillie every night. Neffie even allowed Dillie to groom her with her little pink tongue. When the baby got too close to a tender spot, Neffie would warn her with a playful swipe.

The Abyssinian cat breed is known for its "agouti" brown coat with black ticking, which is identical to the fur of deer or wild rabbits. Abys also have relatively large ears and are fantastic athletes and jumpers, so maybe it made sense that our feline felt a kinship with our deer.

More maternal than Lady, Neffie sometimes groomed her oversize baby with her barbed tongue. She was a great comfort to Dillie, who hated to be alone. With Neffie curled up beside her, she was quiet and content.

Lady and Neffie had never gotten along. When Lady had joined the family five years earlier, the only animals in the house were Neffie and Sally, the cat we found on the doorstep of the emergency clinic. Lady considered chasing the cats one of her daily chores. The first time Lady tried to terrorize Sally, the cat stood her ground and gave Lady an uppercut to the nose, and that was the end of that. Neffie used her Olympic abilities to run, jump, and spring away from Lady, bounding from the floor to the top of the refrigerator. This only convinced Lady that Neffie was a squirrel, and the game escalated.

Our cat Sally had a good, long life and passed away at the age of twenty. She was buried in one of her favorite sunning spots by the swimming pool.

Now that Neffie was Lady's only target, she hated the poodle even more. She disappeared when Lady was in the house. As soon as Lady left with Steve on his daily errands, Neffie wandered from room to room, enjoying her domain. When she heard the chug of the truck's diesel engine, she growled, jumped from her comfy spot, and went into hiding.

When Lady slept at night, the house was Neffie's once again, and she moved around freely. She would climb into bed with the rest of the family, Lady included, and hide under the covers. When the sun came up or the lights went on, Neffie would bolt under the bed so fast that Lady never realized her archrival had just spent the night beside her.

Neffie was completely at ease with Dillie. Even if she didn't know what the new critter was, she knew it wasn't a dog.

Neffie and Lady had seen all sorts of creatures come through the house: rabbits, raccoons, foxes, hawks, owls, songbirds, ducks, and even an occasional fawn had spent days and nights with us as we nursed them back to health for the wildlife rehabilitators. None of them ever moved in for good, though. They all went back to the wild.

Years before Dillie came into our lives, wildlife officers brought us a two-week-old buck whose mother had been hit by a car. Today, it is no longer legal to help injured or abandoned wild fawns. The strict laws were based on the fear of spreading chronic wasting disease. We called the fawn Rudy in honor of my grandmother Rose's husband, who had passed away recently. We were instructed to bottle feed the baby, because he was too young for solid food. The deer spent nights outside. The wildlife people hoped that a doe in the wild herd in the area would adopt him and foster him, so he would stop coming for his bottle. That did not happen. He had to be fed canned goat milk to stay alive. If we called Rudy's name, he would trot out of the woods, walk into the house, and head straight for the refrigerator where the formula was kept.

After about a year, a big buck with one antler came out of the woods and challenged Rudy, who stood his ground. Not long after the encounter, Rudy disappeared. We saw him hanging out with other bucks, which was appropriate for his age.

Several neighbors came to our door asking where Rudy had gone. We were surprised to learn that Rudy had liked to drop in on the neighbors to watch TV in the evening when we thought he was roaming the woods.

Lady and Neffie had known Rudy, but Dillie was different. Raising her was a family affair. Steve took care of the bottle-feeding and exercise, and I handled the medical needs. Lady was her companion in the yard, and Neffie was her bedtime buddy. With the help of her new family, Dillie felt loved every moment of the day and night, and she quickly became a permanent fixture.

A few weeks later, boosted by her newfound confidence and strength, Dillie soon realized the planks around her straw bed could not contain her. She had places to go. When Steve placed her in her bed one morning for her nap, she head-butted the boards out of her way and followed the sound of his footsteps to the door. If Neffie wasn't there to keep her company, she would just stay with Papa.

Dillie's little hoof steps were so quiet that Steve didn't notice she was just three paces behind him when he entered the house. With her impaired vision and lack of experience of the world around her, Dillie knew nothing about open and closed doors. There was a heavy thud. She had hit the glass with such force that she fell, splay-legged, Bambi-on-ice style. Steve threw open the door and found her dazed and down.

"Dillie! What were you thinking?" he asked, scooping her up in his arms.

She licked his face and nibbled at his ear. She had achieved her goal. All she had wanted was to stay with her papa and enjoy the warmth and security of his arms.

From that point on, Dillie had free rein inside the house and the fenced-in yard. During the day, she followed Steve everywhere he went. If he had to leave the house, he would leave Lady with Dillie, and she'd follow the poodle instead. Lady had come to tolerate and even comfort the fawn.

I watched Dillie and Lady playing a kind of tag from

the bedroom window. Dillie, hot on Lady's heels, bumped into her. Lady spun around, growled, and charged at the fawn. The fawn leaped backward. Lady then ran away from Dillie, who took off after her. I was delighted.

In the evening, the family adjourned to the living room to watch television on the sectional sofa. Steve and I sat on the right-hand side, and Lady lay on the corner triangular piece. Steve picked up Dillie and placed her between us, where she relaxed. Neffie stayed away.

Dillie was the baby of the family, but the baby was no longer so little. She was in the middle of a growth spurt, and quickly went from being smaller than Neffie to as tall as Lady. In just a few weeks, her legs had doubled in length.

Agile as Ginger Rogers, she sprang onto the sectional sofa on her own the evening after she bumped into the door. Instead of sitting between Steve and me on the right side of the couch, she leaped onto the corner pillow and nuzzled next to Lady. Dillie had claimed her seat on the sofa, where she sat almost anytime we watched TV.

Dillie didn't understand she was a different species from the rest of us. She did not know she was supposed to fear humans and dogs. All she knew was that we were a family—her family. She wanted, needed, to be with us all the time because of the love we shared.

Dillie's job was to return our love, with interest.

Chapter 9

The Carolina Reaper

I've moonlighted at veterinary emergency clinics that tackle only a few cases each night. If they treat five cases a night, they think they're busy; ten cases are unheard of.

My clinic was not like that. After twenty years of growth, we were busy, sometimes overwhelmingly so. I dedicated half my life to the Stark County Veterinary Emergency Clinic. I volunteered there in high school, when it was just a desk and a few kennels. When I took over in 1989, the clinic was still tiny, unprofitable, and struggling to stay open. By the time Dillie joined our little family in 2004, we had expanded into a 7,000-square-foot facility. I personally had cared for more than 300,000 cases. Sometimes it felt as if all 300,000 came in on a single night.

A typical night at the clinic included ten inpatients

requiring ICU monitoring, a few puppies in isolation with the extremely serious and highly contagious intestinal parvo virus, and twenty or so new patients arriving with various illnesses or injuries, accompanied by pet parents displaying different states of sanity and duress.

I compared nights at the ER to the Scoville scale, which measures the intensity of chili peppers. A jalapeño was rated at 1,000 units, a habanero at 100,000. Ghost peppers were a staggering 1,000,000 units, and the Carolina Reaper, the mother of all hot peppers, was a near-death experience at 2,000,000 units. Using this scale, a regular night at the clinic was a piquant jalapeño, a busy night a lip-blistering habanero, and a summer holiday night a killer ghost pepper. The Fourth of July of the summer Dillie joined us was a Carolina Reaper, grown by the devil's own gardener.

When I came on duty for the anchor leg of the marathon shift, every kennel in the hospital was full. All twenty isolation kennels housed sick pups with parvo virus. All thirty of the regular kennels were full, and some had to be split in half to house two patients.

Dropping off my purse in the doctor's bedroom, I found a Saint Bernard with pneumonia. In the bathroom, two aquariums housed sick guinea pigs. The staff meeting room held another aquarium, which held a ball python that needed a laceration repaired.

We didn't have time to do rounds that night. As soon as I came on duty, my associate Dr. Eric started one surgery after another: twisted stomachs, C-sections, intestinal foreign bodies. I started working through the cases in the exam rooms and the crowd of patients in the lobby.

I went into the first exam room to see a Brittany spaniel who had been stung by a bee and had a face like a hippo. He was not critical and only needed a couple of injections. As I finished my exam, Sherry tapped on the door.

"We need you," she said.

Looking out the window of the exam room, I could see two more staff members pushing a gurney with a large German shepherd lying on his side. The dog was muzzled and snarling, with good reason. There was a six-inch hole in his chest wall, completely exposing his salmon-pink lungs and beating heart. I told my technician what injections we needed for the Brittany and started to head back to the treatment area with the shepherd. As I did, a woman in the lobby stood up.

"Hey, wait a minute!" she shouted. "We've been waiting over an hour. We're next."

Her shrill voice resounded through the entire hospital. She carried on about her dog, who had been shot in the foot three days ago but needed to be seen immediately. She demanded to speak to the owner of the clinic.

She had seen the shepherd being wheeled right past her, heart visible, body soaked in blood, and before that a greyhound with heatstroke and a temperature of 112 degrees, and a cat with an arrow through its eye.

I kept my cool. "I am the owner. We have to take the patients who are the most critical first." We had signs all over the lobby that stated this. "Your dog has been triaged and is stable. These pets are dying. I promise you, if your dog's heart was hanging out of his chest, he would be next."

I turned to Pat at the front desk and asked her to give

the woman directions to the nearest emergency clinic, thirty miles away.

"No," she said loudly. "I will just take him to my doctor tomorrow. And I will make sure I tell him about how I was treated here."

What a threat! She could have brought her injured pet in at any time during the last three days, or could have taken him to her vet's office in the first place. Her vet was an old friend. Once I told him how the woman had behaved, he might bop her over the head with a rubber hammer in my defense.

The German shepherd was in remarkably good condition for a dog whose pulsing heart was visible. He was in shock, of course, but still alive, which in itself was a miracle. Eric had already slipped in an IV while I dealt with the irate client in the waiting room.

Sherry gave us the history. The dog had been shot at close range with a shotgun by a neighbor. Instead of penetrating the heart, the angle of the blast blew off the chest wall. As it turned out, the neighbor had threatened the dog before, because the shepherd ran loose in the neighborhood and had bitten his little girl.

"They're in there screaming bloody murder," Sherry said, pointing at the lounge. "They are going to sue the neighbor and make them pay and blah, blah, blah."

"Wouldn't it be easier just to keep their dog from running loose?" I asked. Sadly, most of the cases in any veterinary ER could have been prevented with a little common sense, which seems to be in short supply.

The dog's injury was more than our little clinic could

handle. He was going to need reconstructive chest wall surgery at Ohio State, which was going to cost thousands of dollars, maybe tens of thousands.

Eric suggested we fashion a plastic splint over the chest wall with a chest tube and a one-way Heimlich valve to allow air to escape. That would protect the heart and keep air from building into a deadly pneumothorax, collapsing the lungs. Once the dog was stable, the clients could transport him to OSU.

Eric busied himself with his chest wall splint invention, and I went to talk to the clients.

As Sherry had warned me, they were furious at their neighbor. I tried to ignore their agitation and concentrate on informing them that the injury required some very advanced, aggressive, and expensive treatment.

Money was not an issue, they told me. "Our neighbor is going to pay for this. Even if we have to take him to court."

They were too upset to listen to logic. I tried anyway. "You may have to take them to court to reimburse you for the costs, but you will have to pay for the services first and hope the court finds in your favor."

I had to leave my explanation at that, because Sherry tapped on the door again.

"We need you," she said.

A client had come in screaming that her dog had been hit by a car and wasn't breathing. As I reached the front desk, the staff wheeled out a gurney to transport the dog.

We followed the latest frantic client to the parking lot. She had pulled into the lot so hard and fast that her front bumper was touching the brick of the building. Her injured dog was in the trunk of her car. When she popped open the trunk, it was clear that the dog had been dead for a while, long enough for flies to have landed on its face and laid eggs. I checked for a heartbeat anyway. The dog was in full rigor, completely stiff. I knew the animal was beyond help, but realized a client this distraught would not accept that her pet was dead unless I checked for a pulse.

"I'm sorry, ma'am," I told her. "He's gone."

"Gone?" she asked. "Gone where?"

This was going to be a long day.

"He's passed away," I said as gently as I could.

"No, he can't be!" she screamed. "You have to do CPR." She was hyperventilating. I was afraid she was going to pass out right there in the lot.

I told Sherry to take the dog to the back and intubate him. We both knew it was absurd, but the parking lot was not the place to rush a hysterical client through the stages of grief.

The woman followed us into the clinic and threw herself down on the tile floor, screaming. Rhonda ran to comfort her, while Sherry and I moved the rigid, long-dead dog to the back.

"Ma'am," Rhonda said in soothing tones, "it will be all right. Everything's going to be all right."

"Whoa," I told Sherry in the back. "That's the most hysterical client I have ever seen."

"You're not really going to do CPR on this dog, are you?" Sherry asked. "Look at him." She rolled him onto his back, and his rigid legs stuck straight up in the air.

"I just need some time for her to calm down so she

can understand that her dog is beyond CPR. He's already decomposing!" This client had to have known her dog was dead, or why would she have put her pet in a trunk to make the thirty-minute trip here?

Rhonda had gotten the woman off the floor and moved her to a couch. She sat holding the woman's hand, trying to prevent her from throwing herself on the floor again.

I bent down in front of her and broke the news as gently as I could. "There is nothing we can do to bring him back to life," I said. "He has been dead for a long time."

She stood up slowly and glared at Rhonda. "You . . . you," she said menacingly. "You told me it would be all right!" She waved an accusatory finger at Rhonda.

Fortunately, the woman's calmer husband, who had come in a separate vehicle, appeared in the doorway and took charge. He had explained to his wife that the dog was dead before she left home, but she had ignored him.

He apologized for the scene she had made and said he would drive her home.

Rhonda and I retreated.

We went through the cases one by one until the lobby was empty. Then we finished the procedures on the patients in the back. The roll call was staggering. In twenty-four hours, we had seen 105 cases, many of them supercritical.

While Eric finished his charts, I sutured up the ball python. The coughing Saint Bernard in the doctor's bedroom was on his way home with antibiotics. About half the parvo pups were well enough to go home, while the rest had to stay for the duration of their treatment. The cooking greyhound had cooled down, stabilized, and was doing well. The cat with the arrow in her eye had somehow survived without losing the eye. The arrow's tip had been sticking out of the bone above the nose, and Eric was able to clip it off and remove the shaft. He had also delivered a dozen golden retriever puppies by C-section, and they were all nestled contentedly against their mama. The German shepherd had been stabilized, and the owners were going to take him to Ohio State that night. The Carolina Reaper night was finally cooling down. The whole building seemed to breathe a sigh of relief.

As we worked through the rest of the cases, I called Steve and suggested he bring some food for the staff. He arrived with pizzas and wings for everyone.

"Wow! You guys have been busy," Steve said as he started doing the laundry and cleaning. He always judged how busy we had been by the amount of laundry there was. Today's pile was eight feet tall. Isolation had its own laundry room, and the parvo pups had produced their own eight-foot pile.

I was in the exam room going over instructions with the owners of the ball python when Sherry tapped on the door, once again.

"We need you," she said.

She ushered me into the second exam cottage, the log cabin. "Six-year-old cat," she told me, "female, spayed. Been vomiting for days. Body temp is ninety-two. Client's name is Millie Reynolds." With a body temperature ten degrees below normal, the cat needed immediate thermal support.

Bundled in a blanket on the table, the cat did not lift her head when I began my exam. The owner, a very elderly lady, was dressed in a housecoat and slippers. She had pulled a chair up next to the exam table and was petting her dying cat with a trembling hand.

"You have to save her, Doc," she said to me as I introduced myself. "She's all I have." Tears streamed down her cheeks.

I handed her a box of Kleenex. "Let's see what's wrong with her. How long has she been sick?"

Millie's cat, Sonja, had been vomiting for five days. Up until then, she had been healthy and was strictly an indoor cat.

"Please save her, Doc," Millie implored.

Sonja was weak from severe dehydration. Her belly was hurting, and her breath reeked of infection. I peered in her mouth and saw a large, infected cut under her tongue. Embedded in the cut was the culprit: a piece of red thread.

Sonja had what is known as a linear foreign body. She had ingested thread, and the thread had caught around her tongue as it passed into the stomach. From there, it had continued to pass into the intestines. Since it was anchored on the tongue, it pulled her intestine into pleats and was beginning to saw through the delicate tissue.

"Have you been sewing?" I asked Millie.

"Oh yes," she answered. "I quilt. I'm working on a quilt for Sonja."

I explained to her what was wrong. Sonja was going to need surgery once we got her stabilized.

"Oh, Doc, I can't do that," she sobbed softly. "I spent

my last dollar on the cab fare over here. I could never afford a surgery."

"Is there anyone who can help you?" I asked. "A family member?"

"No," Millie said quietly. "There's no one. I am alone. Can you save her, Doc? I promise I will pay you, I promise."

Millie bowed her head and stroked her beloved cat. Sick as she was, Sonja purred as she felt the old woman's touch. Millie began to sob again, and Sherry put her arm around the old woman.

I thought of my grandmother Millie, my namesake, who had passed away a few years earlier at ninety-two.

"We will try to save her," I told the owner. "I can't promise anything, but we will try. Sonja will need fluids and surgery, so she'll have to stay here a few days."

Millie's body shook with sobs, and she repeated, "Thank you, Doc. I promise I will pay you. I promise."

We brought the cat to the back and started the IV fluids and electrolytes. We drew blood and snipped the red thread under the tongue, releasing tension on the bowel.

By now, the whole hospital was aware of what had happened in the exam room. Pat came to the back from the front desk and patted me on the shoulder. "You done good, gal," she said.

"Well, good won't pay the bills," I told her.

"Everything you do here is building you a house in heaven," she said. "You just put on a whole roof."

Sonja was stable enough by the middle of the night for us to take her to surgery. About a foot of her small intestine was dead and had to be removed. We had to rebuild her remaining intestine, good end to good end. Sonja bounced back from the physical trauma as if it was nothing. She may have used up a few of her nine lives, but eventually she was able to go home and sleep on her newly made quilt.

A few weeks after the Carolina Reaper night, I received a subpoena for the medical records of the German shepherd. The clients had sued the neighbor for the cost of the surgery at Ohio State plus the usual trumped-up fees for "pain and suffering." The court decided the neighbor had to pay the medical expenses, even though this shepherd had sent his little girl to an emergency room.

The subpoena was soon followed by the first installment on Sonja's $900 bill. Millie had mailed in her first payment, four quarters taped to a pink index card. She had written on the card:

Sonja is doing well. Thank you.

Now her balance was $899. A month after that, another pink index card arrived with four more quarters, and another note from Millie. At this rate, it would take her seventy-four years to pay her bill.

Steve suggested we call her and waive the rest of the bill. He wanted to make the call.

"No," Millie cried when he told her. "I am paying it. I am doing the best I can!"

"You don't understand," Steve said. "Waiving it means you don't have to pay it anymore. It doesn't mean anything bad."

She cried with relief, and thanked us again.

We received one more index card from her. No quarters this time, just a note.

Dear Doctor,
    Thank you for saving my Sonja. Bless you.
    I ask God every night to look after you.
           You are my angel, always.

Of the 105 cases we saw on the Carolina Reaper, Sonja's was the most rewarding one. Except for the eight quarters, Millie's bill was paid in blessings, not cash.

Chapter 10

~~~~~

Dillie Goes Off the Deep End

I woke up exhausted after the grueling night. Since I didn't have to go into work later that day, I joined our family in their ritual walk around the yard. Even Neffie decided to tag along on the trek. She didn't want Lady to see her and chase her back into the house. Instead of marching in the parade, the little cat crept behind us, dodging from bush to bush, staying hidden but always within a few feet of us. Neffie's maternal friendship with Dillie had emboldened her. Our shy cat was more open to spending time with the rest of the family, cuddling with Steve and me, but she would still scamper off when Lady got too curious.

Dillie, now a few months old, stood shoulder to shoulder with Lady. She was going through nearly five cans of goat's milk a day and growing fast. Dillie and Lady were playing tug-of-war by the pool with one of Lady's many stuffed animals, which were strewn all over the yard. Lady was very protective of her toys. When she went outside, she brought her toys, one at a time. At night, Lady scratched at the door to go out—not to do her business, but to find the toys she had left in the yard. A few seconds later, she came back, first toy retrieved. She placed that toy on the couch with care, and then headed back outside for the next. She repeated this activity until either all the toys were back where they belonged, or one of us finally said, "That's enough, Lady!"

Tug-of-war started when Dillie sniffed the ground and discovered a stuffed teddy bear, lion, or other critter. Curious, she licked the toy and pushed it with her nose. Lady was not about to let Dillie take her toys. Whenever Lady saw Dillie playing with one of her belongings, she charged over, snatched it back, and carried it to the safe zone under the picnic table. By the end of any given day, the picnic table had become a stuffed-toy bomb shelter.

As the toy was being yanked out from under her nose, Dillie extended a long, thin leg and pinned the teddy bear to the ground with a dainty hoof. Her defiance provoked Lady to redouble her efforts to retrieve the toy. After a few seconds, Dillie became more interested in licking Lady than stomping on the toy. As Lady moved the toy back to the bunker, Dillie jumped up in the air, all four feet leaving the ground at the same time. Always playful, Dillie was getting into the game.

Steve and I laughed from our front-row seats at the picnic table.

Steve began sweeping up the fallen seedpods and berries

around the pool. Dillie looked up and suddenly realized that Steve was more than a few feet away. She made a beeline for him. Unfortunately, that straight line took her right into the swimming pool.

When we heard the splash, we turned to look and saw Dillie completely submerged in eight feet of water. She had fallen into the deep end.

"Dillie!" I screamed.

Steve dropped the rake, and we both dove into the pool from opposite ends. We swam frantically in our clothes and shoes to reach her.

Dillie's head popped right up as if nothing unusual had happened, and she began to swim like an Olympic gold medalist. She used her long legs like oars, stroking her way through the water. She was completely unafraid. In fact, she was enjoying it!

We watched, amazed, as Dillie swam around the pool. I knew that white-tailed deer are usually adept swimmers, who can reach speeds of up to ten miles per hour, swift enough to beat Michael Phelps. But I was worried that Dillie's blindness and inexperience might affect her ability to swim.

Dripping wet, the cell phone in my pocket ruined, I felt a little foolish.

"She could give swimming lessons to children," I said to Steve.

"I know," said Steve. "It's like she was born to swim."

As we walked over to the steps to get out of the pool, Dillie followed us right up the three broad steps. She shook like a dog after a bath, showering Lady with spray in the process. Lady proclaimed her irritation with a loud, sharp bark. Though poodles had been developed to be water dogs, Lady hated the pool. She hated baths. She hated the hose. She hated rain. The only water she liked was in her dish. The few times she accidentally fell into the pool she flailed her way to the poolside and churned water until Steve helped her out. She would have drowned if he had not rescued her. I wondered if Lady was jealous of Dillie's swimming prowess as much as getting soaked annoyed her.

I ran into the house to change and to dry out my damaged cell phone. Steve threw off his wet shoes and shirt and dove back into the pool.

Dillie stood alert at the pool's edge, prepared to jump in and rescue him if necessary. Then she made her way down the steps and into the water to join him. By the time Steve had reached the end of his lap, Dillie was beside him in the deep end.

"What are you doing, little one?" he asked her.

She swam calmly in a circle, staying close. And when Steve headed back to the shallow end, his hooved shadow was a few strokes behind him.

I stood and watched Steve and Dillie swimming side by side.

"What the heck . . . ," I muttered.

A little water was not going to keep Dillie from Steve. After watching them doing laps, I jumped in and joined them.

When Steve and I climbed out of the pool, Dillie was a few steps behind us. As we grabbed towels, she shook herself dry. This time, Lady stayed away.

Dillie became a frequent pool-mate for Steve. Sometimes she went into the pool on her own, wading down the steps, swimming a few laps, then climbing up and out, with a shake. She preferred playing in the shallow end, which was still deep for a fawn, to swimming laps with us. So we did something that was a first in our years of animal rescue: We bought Dillie a kiddie pool. She splashed around in it for hours, sometimes picking up the hose and spraying water all around, while Lady watched from a safe distance.

Chapter 11

The House Deer

By the end of that first summer, Dillie had begun to lose her baby spots and was getting lanky. In the wild, she would have been following her mother and learning appropriate deer behavior and feeding patterns. Dillie had to make due with our interspecies herd, but she was thriving, growing heavier every day.

By October, when the leaves were turning color and beginning to fall, Dillie's spots had disappeared. One morning I saw her transform her favorite swimming hole into a huge green trampoline. She bounded out onto our pool cover, bounced straight up, and then slid in the water that collected when she weighed the cover down. Wherever she stood, the water gathered on the cover and followed her.

"Dillie!" I shouted. "That's not safe!" Expecting her to

tear through the fabric and get trapped beneath it, I ran to the pool. The cover supported Dillie's weight just fine. She flashed her white tail at me, then catapulted straight into the air before landing in a puddle. She splashed and played, delighting in the game.

Her vision was still impaired, but as she grew, her eyes did, too. The cataracts stayed the same size and took up proportionately less of her visual field. The improvement in her vision made her even bolder and more adventurous.

When Dillie, Steve, Lady, and Neffie, still sneaking behind, would go on their daily walks, Dillie discovered new sounds and smells, like the rustle of the leaves and the earthy smell of autumn. She tasted, played with, or consumed every leaf she found on the ground. They walked the fence line and visited the horses every day. Dillie was now used to the clip-clop of horse hooves and didn't run away when she heard it, but she still refused to approach the fence to meet the horses. Although they wanted to befriend her, Dillie wouldn't let them get near enough to try, but Lady was undaunted. She was bold enough to steal a carrot from Kibbles's mouth as he hung his head over the fence.

Dillie still drank Meyenberg's goat milk every day, but she had started to eat hay, grain, and any plant she found. She was growing like a weed, though no weed in our yard got to grow very tall before she ate it. Every shrub, bush, and tree was under attack. The butterfly bushes that surrounded the pool were stripped bare. They would not survive the winter. The young weeping cherry looked more like a palm tree, its upright branches cropped where Dillie had gnawed as high as she could reach.

Dillie was also exploring inside the house, where she trailed Lady from room to room. As I was working in my office one day, I heard a cacophony of sound coming from downstairs. I went down to investigate and found Dillie banging away on the piano with her nose. She seemed to be enjoying the racket she was making.

She became adept at opening kitchen cabinets with her mouth and foraging for treats. Boxes and bags were no challenge. She shook their contents all over the kitchen floor. We had to store food in Dillie-proof containers in the lower cabinets.

She even followed Lady outside to relieve herself, and when she couldn't get outside, she went on a mat spread out by her straw corral in the garage. Dillie house-trained herself. Wild does go to great lengths to make sure that their fawns' droppings do not alert predators to their location. Sometimes they even eat the scat. Dillie may have been naturally inclined to do her business outside.

When Steve and I left the house to run errands, we put Dillie in her corral. She slept there at night and seemed more comfortable in the corral than in other parts of the house, even though she still maintained her spot on the couch.

One day, when Dillie was just an inch or two taller than Lady, we came home to find the garage empty.

"Where the heck could she have gone?" Steve asked.

"She's got to be around here somewhere," I said. "A deer can't just disappear!"

We searched each room on the ground floor. Tail wagging, Lady came downstairs with a stuffed cow in her mouth to greet us, but Dillie was nowhere to be found. In our quiet little town, we never needed to lock the back door, but a flash of fear came over us. "You don't think that someone might have come in, do you?" Steve asked.

"That's just not possible." I was puzzled. "I'm going to check upstairs."

"She doesn't know how to go up steps," Steve said, and then anxiously started to search the first floor again, checking under the furniture.

Dillie routinely climbed out of the pool, but it had only three steps and the water served as a buffer if she fell. The bedrooms, on the other hand, were up a long, steep flight of steps.

At the top of the staircase I turned the corner and there, in our bedroom, stood one very proud, eighty-pound fawn, right in the middle of the bed.

"She's up here!" I called to Steve, relieved.

When Steve appeared at my side, Dillie jumped off the bed and went to lick his hands.

"How did she get up those stairs?" he wondered.

"Beats me," I answered. "But it looks like she's been licking your pillow for hours." I pointed at the sopping pillow on his side of the bed.

"Sixty, you have been a busy girl!" She licked his hand. "Let's see how you handle going down the stairs."

Dillie started down the stairs fearlessly, one small black hoof at a time. She coordinated the front and back legs perfectly: front foot, back foot, front foot, back foot. We watched in amazement.

"That's a good girl, Dillie," Steve said, beaming.

At bedtime that evening, there was no containing Dillie in the straw corral. We left the door to the garage open a crack as usual, but she pushed through and went right up the stairs and jumped on our bed as if she owned it.

Our sturdy, Amish-made, four-poster bed was now holding not only the two of us, hardly known for our diminutive size, but also a sixty-five-pound standard poodle, a seven-pound Abyssinian cat, and a still-growing, eighty-pound doe.

Dillie chose her position carefully, as close as she could to Papa. She stood between Steve and me and slowly folded one front leg under her, then the other. Next, she lowered her caboose, and the bed bounced as she plopped down. I feigned disgust as Dillie licked Steve's face. How had our reasonably normal lives come to this?

"Dillie, no!" Steve said. "You have to let me sleep!" He pushed her toward the middle of the bed, and she turned to me, kissing my face and hair as I tried to squirm away. Her thick tongue was agile and smooth, and very wet. After I was thoroughly doused, she turned back to Steve, who was trying to keep her off his pillow.

If she couldn't lay her head on Steve's pillow, she chose the next best thing, his chest. From that vantage point, she could gaze up at my husband with loving eyes.

He tried to push Dillie's head away as she kept licking his chin and face.

"I can't believe this. I think it's time to move her to the barn." As I said it, I knew full well that this move would never happen. I sighed and tried to get comfortable on a mattress crowded with our poodle, cat, and deer. The first night was rough, but I got used to it. In time, I came to love the feel of Dillie pressed up against me.

Dillie was now a house deer.

Chapter 12

Al Dente for Dillie

The family bed became even more crowded as Dillie grew. There was no denying her. The only place she ever wanted to be was within a nose's length of Steve. If he went out of her sight for even a second, her tan forehead would crinkle with anxiety. If he went outside without her, she would stand at the back door, nose pressed against the full-length window, waiting. She would not relax until Steve's diesel engine chugged back up the driveway.

Wild fawns imprint on their mothers, or a reasonable substitute, and live in small herds with them. Does stay with their mothers and the other females, and bucks form herds of their own. In our household, the best substitute doe was probably Lady, but Dillie chose Steve.

I think that Dillie looks at me as a sister, or maybe an

aunt. She is very fond of me, kissing me whenever I come near, and enjoys curling up with Lady and me. I love to stroke her coat, which has two layers, like a Siberian husky: a coarse outer one and a downy under coat. Wild deer shed their coat down to the velvety under layer during the summer, but since Dillie lives inside, her shedding isn't strictly seasonal. She sheds every nine months or so, typically when summer turns to fall. Deer in the wild shed their winter coats in spring so they can stay cool through the summer.

Watching Dillie and Steve together is endlessly entertaining, especially when Steve cooks. When Steve prepares a large salad of mixed greens, fruits, and various grains for Dillie, she tugs at the red-speckled, enamel-coated metal platter that serves as her feeding dish. She licks her nose and Steve's hands as he chops the fruit. She has her hay, but from the day she stopped drinking goat's milk, she has explored every food item she could. She loves nearly all fruits, especially berries, apples, and pears. But bananas are her favorite. Sometimes she helps herself to one, pulling the individual fruit off the bunch on the counter. She usually snags one with her lips, grips it in her teeth, and then tosses her head up, separating the banana, or at least a portion of it, from the rest. She eats them peel and all.

Now that Dillie's head is level with the kitchen island where we eat, our meals are in peril. If we eat something, she wants to try it, too. She grabs the edge of our plates and pulls them toward her. If we do not share what we are eating with her, she bobs her head up and down, licks her nose, and sniffs until we do. I thought a poodle could disrupt the dinner table, but Dillie is a much more persistent beggar than Lady. There is no stopping her if she really wants to try something. Either we share or she takes the food right off our plates.

One morning, Steve picked me up after I had worked a very long weekend. I could barely stay awake in the car. When we got home, Lady ran up to me with a toy, to play hide-and-seek. "Not today, girl," I said, giving her a pat on the head. I was too tired to play with Lady, much less share the bed with Dillie. I chased Dillie out of the bed and crashed. Neffie, curled up under the blankets, was a bit less invasive than a deer. I fell asleep as she purred at my feet.

After getting kicked out of her comfy bed, Dillie wandered downstairs to see what Steve was up to. Since I worked such long hours, Steve became the head family cook. He wasn't a fancy chef by any means, but he could turn out a decent array of man meals: barbecue, steak, chili, grilled cheese sandwiches, and spaghetti. Since I had a rare night off, Steve wanted to wake me up to a special dinner of linguine and a beautiful salad.

As Steve washed the lettuce, Dillie tried to sample the cucumbers, tomatoes, onions, and mushrooms piled on the counter. She snaked her head over the counter and grabbed whichever vegetable Steve did not have in his hands. Finally, Steve gave her a little plate of bananas and pears to keep her busy so that he could slice the vegetables. He was barely through the cucumbers before Dillie snapped up some snow peas with her tongue.

Steve put a pot of water on the stove, and then he, Lady, and Dillie climbed the stairs to wake me. I had already been awake for about an hour, listening to the commotion in the kitchen. *Chop. Chop.* "Dillie, get out of here!" *Slice. Slice.* "Now, Dillie, leave me alone! I am trying to get this done for Mom!"

Steve came up to ask if I was ready to eat. Both Lady and Dillie, who weighed more than a hundred pounds at that point, jumped on the bed, springing me to an upright position.

"Guess so," I replied.

I cooked spaghetti the way my Sicilian grandmothers had taught me, by testing the noodles to see if they were *al dente*. Steve timed his spaghetti. Exactly ten minutes later, the steaming noodles were served onto plates, and we sat down to eat. I liked a spoonful of marinara on top of linguine, but Steve liked his with butter and a lot of pepper. After serving me, he turned to get the pepper grinder.

That was when Dillie made her move. She was so quick that she had nearly his entire serving of linguine in her mouth by the time Steve turned back around. Strands of pasta hung down from both sides of her delicate mouth. She slurped the rest up, finishing off the few pieces she had left behind, as Steve stood motionless, pepper grinder in hand.

Dillie was not done. She tried to steal my serving, too.

"Stop that, Dillie," Steve said, grabbing the tongs and serving Dillie her own linguine, so she would let us eat in peace.

"We have a Sicilian deer," Steve announced.

"Better not make her mad!"

Spaghetti became the other great love of Dillie's life.

Chapter 13

Room for One More

I sold the emergency clinic in August 2004. Selling the clinic was my attempt to retire and relax, probably for the first time in my adult life. Our family expanded again as a result of the sale. Spazz, the clinic cat, joined us. The new owners had let go of nearly all the employees, including Sherry, Pat, Angie and Shawna. Spazz's job was terminated, too.

Spazz had become a valuable asset to the clinic because he donated blood, thanks to his generous size and correspondingly large blood volume. Despite his gender, he had an inclination to mother orphaned kittens, allowing them to nestle in his thick fur for warmth and security. His most important duty was to be the client comforter-in-chief. When a pet owner was distraught, Spazz went to the lobby, climbed on the client's lap, if allowed, and comforted the worried human. Many clients were so touched by this gesture that they actually took the time to send thank-you notes addressed to "Spazz, the Clinic Cat."

After a decade of dedicated service to the clinic, his clinic, I placed the huge, squirming cat into a plastic container to transport him to our place.

"Time for you to retire, big guy," I told him. "You're going to be a gentleman farmer."

I gave Spazz a room away from the other animals until he got used to his surroundings and set up a space for him in a guest bedroom. He had all the feline essentials in there: food, water, litter box, and a large bed with soft comforters for him to snuggle in and knead with his claws. He already knew Lady from her daily visits to the clinic, and he had long ago taught her to keep a safe distance from his claws, which rivaled Freddy Krueger's knife-fingered glove. When we brought Spazz home, Lady ran up to sniff the carrier. It took only one warning swipe for her to respect Spazz's boundaries, whether it was her house or not.

When Dillie strode into the room, Spazz froze. He didn't know whether to run away, ignore her, or attack. He jumped onto the bed, tail down and back coiled, and watched her, ready to spring away or strike if she threatened him.

Dillie's impaired vision forced her to explore the world mainly through scents, taste, and touch. She didn't have fingers, but she had a very useful replacement: her tongue. With that tool, she could not only feel what she was exploring but also taste it. She approached Spazz and began to lick him.

From the first lick, Spazz understood that Dillie was placed on Earth to be his personal groomer. He no longer had to stretch to groom himself. Dillie was reaching places on his head and neck he could not even have hoped to get to. Spazz seemed to believe that every worldly item was created for the sole purpose of pleasing him.

Spazz stretched out on the soft bed and let Dillie groom his head, belly, and neck. He was quick with a gentle swat, claws retracted, to teach her to avoid sensitive areas like his back.

Watching them, I called to Steve, "I think this is going to work out! They are already best buddies." In reality, or at least the feline version of it, they were more like master and servant.

Spazz didn't seem to bother anybody except the usually placid Neffie. Abyssinians look very much like miniature cougars, often with an attitude equal to their full-size cousins. Neffie followed Dillie into the room to see what the commotion was about. Her ornery side had never appeared before, but she took one look at Spazz, and the genetic switch flipped. She let out a scream, a hiss, and a yowl that would have stopped an American buffalo in its tracks. Lady barked at the tiny cat, who had suddenly found her voice.

Frightened, Dillie fluffed up her tail and body and stomped her foot. She didn't know what was wrong, but she was on instant alert, ready to bolt.

Spazz took one look at the roaring, spitting, hissing, growling, ferocious mini-cougar, twelve pounds below his fighting weight, and yawned. He didn't even bother to fluff up his stubby tail.

Neffie retreated to her bedroom. Although not afraid of Neffie, Spazz respected her space and tried not to challenge her domain. He remained in his room day and night for the first week. Gradually, he began to explore the house and farm and joined the daily visit to the horses with the rest of the crew.

When Dillie was in the yard, Spazz followed her. Whenever he needed a quick groom, he plopped down in front of her, and she would oblige. After being cooped up in the clinic for nearly a decade, Spazz delighted in the green grass and summer sun. He rolled and purred, stretching his legs up to the sky. There was so much to do and see. An entire barn filled with mice to catch. Fences to climb and walk along. Birds to chatter at. He was the cat he was meant to be.

After a long day playing in the yard, Spazz curled up in the main bedroom on the bed with the rest of the family. Humans and animals jostled for space.

"I think we need a bigger bed," Steve said.

"Or smaller animals," I answered as Dillie wedged herself between us, using her hooves to push me aside. "Thank God the horses stay in the barn."

Chapter 14

The Urban Legend

After selling the emergency clinic, Steve and I took a long-overdue vacation. We couldn't imagine who would take on such a huge responsibility for the time we would be away. And then it occurred to me that we knew just the person. Carol Zeh, my high school journalism teacher and old friend, could handle all combinations of animals with aplomb. Zeh was trusted, reliable, a naturalist, and a true animal person. She had what it took to satisfy my overly nervous husband and me. For Zeh's part, staying at our house provided her with a mini-vacation. She chose to live a minimalist lifestyle, so our large pool, wide-screen TV with satellite channels, and washer/dryer were big draws.

Dillie and the cats stayed at home with Zeh, while Steve,

Lady, and I traveled by clunky RV to all four corners of the country for six wonderful weeks. We dreamed of retiring from our family business and moving to northern Idaho. Years earlier, we had purchased land there in the mountains near Lake Pend Oreille, one of the prettiest spots in the country. I hoped to practice there once we moved.

We planned a visit to the property on our RV journey. But everything was different now that Dillie was in our lives. The recently changed Ohio deer laws prohibited farm deer from crossing state lines. If we moved to Idaho, Dillie could not come. We couldn't give her to someone else to raise. When we adopted her, we made a commitment to her for her entire life. We had to postpone our relocation indefinitely, but that's never bothered us. Dillie brings so much to our lives.

We returned rested from our trip and settled into our retirement. I could sleep in my own bed every night, which I had not been able to do for more than two decades. For the first time in our marriage, Steve and I had all our evenings together. I was no longer pushing myself through seventy-two-hour ER shifts, or trying to save four critical patients at once. I was no longer living on adrenaline and caffeine. I found that I didn't have regular clothes to wear. Never a fashion maven, I only had scrubs in my closet. I had dressed in my uniform day and night.

After working an average of a hundred hours a week for nearly half my life, I found myself on a permanent vacation . . . and I was miserable. From the time I was nine years old, all I had ever wanted to be was a veterinarian. Now I had no clinic, no patients. My skills, knowledge, and experience were useless. I could be saving pets' lives, diagnosing diseases, delivering puppies, but here I was, idle and useless.

Steve could not comprehend my restlessness. We argued about it. He caught me one night writing a résumé to send to an emergency clinic in a different city.

"Why can't you just enjoy your retirement?" he asked, exasperated. After waiting two decades for us to have time to do things together, he was upset that a life of leisure wasn't for me. He could see that I was lost without my work.

As I often say, being a vet is not what I do but who I am. Now, without my work, what was I?

I felt bad that my need to work was keeping Steve from living his dreams, but I was too young to retire. I started moonlighting from time to time at local practices, but it just wasn't enough.

I knew my old friend and colleague Dean would understand. I invited him to a barbecue to celebrate my first Labor Day off in twenty years. I wanted to talk to him about the emptiness I felt. He had retired from his own practice a few years earlier, in his mid-fifties, and was experiencing the same void I was.

I have known hundreds of vets in my lifetime. I have had the privilege to study under and work with some of the most respected and well-known vets in the world, the "stars" of my profession. I have never known a vet who had Dean's skill, compassion, and profound connection with animals. God sent Dean to Earth to care for His creatures, and the animals knew it. Snarling dogs that no one could approach would lie down in submission at his feet.

I witnessed Dean perform one of the most difficult tasks on an aggressive dog, a toenail trim. Panzer, a Rottweiler, who weighed in at a hundred pounds, was a seriously aggressive animal. I have combat-style flashbacks involving Rottweilers, and I guarantee that I am not the only vet who has nearly lost body parts to this breed. Rottweilers can be licking and kissing a vet's face, and as soon as they feel a twinge of pain or an ounce of fear, they become canine Terminators. Their strength and size makes them impossible to control. They are often accompanied by owners who refuse to acknowledge the aggressiveness of their dogs, even when they are snapping like grizzly bears at any scrubs-wearing target.

I admitted Panzer to the clinic for a simple nail trim because we were going to have to sedate him to do it. In the exam room, despite his owner's insistence that he would not bite, Panzer lunged at the stupefied owner when he saw the blue nylon muzzle in my hands. I brought Panzer back to a kennel. My plan was to use a rabies pole to keep the dog's snarling head six feet away from us while we injected him with a sedative, then cut his nails.

The rabies pole is an extreme measure reserved for the most dangerous dogs. Only a few dogs in my career have been so threatening that I turned to the pole. One was a huge wolf hybrid, weighing more than his frail, elderly owner, who brought the injured dog to the emergency clinic without a leash. As soon as I entered the exam room, the dog leaped four feet and grabbed my arm at the elbow, shearing it. That dog would have amputated my left arm if my staff hadn't come into the room that instant with the rabies pole. He let go of my arm just long enough to attack the pole. I left Panzer in the kennel room to draw up the sedative.

When I returned to the kennel, syringe in hand, I was shocked to find Dean inside the kennel with Panzer.

"Dean, get out of there!" I whispered. "That dog is an extreme caution." Climbing into a cage with a dog this dangerous was like jumping into a shark tank with a great white.

"No, he's doing okay. I'm almost done," Dean said, hushing me.

Even though I was fully aware of Dean's gift with animals, I was astonished. There he was crouched beside this ferocious Rottweiler, who was extending his paw to Dean. Dean trimmed one nail at a time, without incident.

Sherry joined me with the rabies pole in her hand.

"Now, don't you bite Dr. Dean," he said calmly to the dog. "One more. We're almost done. What a good boy you are, Panzer."

Thousands of stories like this had earned Dean a nickname at my clinic: The Urban Legend. There was something more at play with Dean than just skill. He was a good vet, but so was I. He was compassionate, but so was I. He had a gentle touch with the patients, but so did I. The difference was that Dean had magic. His presence could calm any animal.

He was good with people as well as with their pets. I was in the lobby of the emergency clinic one day when a client named Kim rushed in and told us that her house had burned down and that one of her seven dogs had perished. She was bringing us the other dogs to check for injuries. She waved her bandaged, burnt hands and described how she had rushed into the burning house herself to rescue her dogs. She refused to go to the hospital until her dogs were treated. Her six dogs swirled around her barking and yapping.

When Kim came in, Dean was in the surgery room spaying a cat. He pulled off his gloves, came to the front desk, and hugged Kim without saying a word. Kim, nearly a foot taller than Dean, laid her head on his shoulder and sobbed.

I've thought about that profound gesture so many times since then. I was listening to Kim, and I was feeling her pain, but I would never have hugged her like that.

In my post-retirement funk, I had begun to fantasize about starting a new clinic with Dean. We would keep it small and simple and work only a few days a week. We would keep practicing but still have a life outside of work. Dean was moving into our town, so we could pick a place just a few minutes away from each of us. His family had owned land for generations just down the street from me, and he was building a new house there.

I invited Dean and his wife, Joan, and my former staff members to our Labor Day barbecue. I wanted to spend the afternoon convincing them that we should start a clinic together.

Sherry and her mother, Pat, were the first to arrive. They had worked for me for nearly a decade at the emergency clinic. My future assistant and receptionist were excited about being a team again. They immediately went to work on Steve as he lit the charcoal fire. They were assuring him that we could do this without giving up our family time the way we had at the emergency clinic.

"We will just keep this very small," Sherry told him. "It won't be a hundred hours a week anymore. Just an eight-to-five practice."

"I know her, Sherry," he said. "She can't do anything small."

By the time Dean and Joan arrived, Steve had reluctantly given us his blessing. He knew that I would not be happy until I was working again, and he was glad familiar faces were involved.

Right there by the pool, with steaks sizzling, Dillie trying to tip over our glasses of iced tea, and Lady repeatedly bringing Dean a slobbery toy to throw, Dean and I planned our next clinic.

The Urban Legend was on board.

Chapter 15

From the ER to General Practice

Almost a year to the day since I had left the demands of the emergency clinic, Dean and I began practicing together at Elm Ridge Animal Hospital. Dillie was a yearling, but not yet a star. Very few people in our little town even knew her name, except for the clerks at the local grocery store where we bought her daily supply of endive, bananas, and apples.

Elm Ridge started very modestly in a small storefront. The entire floorplan could have fit easily into the lobby of the emergency clinic I used to own. Our crew consisted of Sherry, her mother Pat, Dean, and his assistant Michele from his previous practice, and me. Our aim was to keep our operation small and efficient.

I planned to work every day, but Dean wanted to work

two days a week so that he could enjoy his semi-retirement. Although I had a solid reputation as an emergency vet, most of the pet owners in our town already had a family vet. Since it would take years for me to build up a substantial client base, we hoped that Dean's former clients would follow him to our clinic.

The night before we opened, I received a call at home from one of Dean's longtime clients.

"I heard Dr. LeBeau is practicing again," she said somewhat breathlessly. "Is he there now?"

"No, "I answered. "It's ten at night, and it's Sunday. He will be there tomorrow."

She started to cry. "I can't believe it," she said through her tears. "I have been praying he would come out of retirement. Praying and praying."

Dean's clients were obsessively devoted to him. Many clients would not let any other vet touch their pets. I knew some of his clients would never warm up to me, but I hoped that enough of them would tolerate me long enough for me to gain their trust.

Not all of them were polite about the prospect.

Just a few weeks after we opened, one of his clients rushed in with her shih tzu, whose left eye was shut. When she discovered Dean was not working that day, she let loose with profanities that were surprising to hear coming from the cherry red mouth of an elderly lady with a one-foot-tall, strawberry blonde, beehive hairdo. She didn't apologize for her expletives and demanded that Pat call Dean to ask him to come in.

"This is an emergency!" she said, pounding her fist on the reception desk.

"Well," Pat was quick to respond, "You're lucky. Dr. Butera is here, and she's worked for more than twenty years doing nothing but emergencies. She's just the lady you should see."

Sitting at the microscope in the back room, I heard the commotion. I went to the lobby to greet the client. "I can take a look at him for you," I said. As I reached to take the dog from her, she spun away, protecting him with her body. "No one holds Rocky but me," she said.

Though I had witnessed her handing her dog to Dean a dozen times, I knew not to argue. I guided her to the exam room and began my exam while she held Rocky. I had to numb Rocky's eye to examine it, because he was keeping it tightly closed out of pain. When I told the client what I was going to do, her response was predictable.

"Is that what Dean would do?"

We became familiar with that refrain. Curtis, who joined us later, grew so tired of hearing this question he created a wristband that read "WWDD," What Would Dean Do?

Once Rocky's eye was numb from the proparacaine drops, he finally opened it. I instilled a fluorescent stain to demonstrate a corneal injury and saw a very large, deep, and dangerous corneal ulcer. If the bacteria causing this ulcer melted just one more speck of cornea, the eye would rupture.

I wanted to refer Rocky to a veterinary ophthalmologist. No matter what Dean, I, or anyone did, this eye could easily rupture and might require surgery. Rocky could lose his eye. As openly hostile as the client had already been, this could be a no-win situation. Distrustful, hostile clients are often appeased by seeing a specialist. I asked Pat to make a few calls. We soon discovered that every veterinary ophthalmologist within a hundred miles was at a national ophthalmology convention. I was on my own for this one.

I told the owner that we had to be very aggressive in treating this condition. I needed to draw some blood from Rocky. If we took plasma from his own blood and treated the eye with it throughout the day, we would douse the ulcer site with healing proteins. "I just need to take him in back and draw some blood."

"No one holds him but me," she repeated.

Sherry tried to soothe her and explained that we would just have him in the back for a few minutes, but the owner only clutched him closer.

"I wish Dean were here," she said.

Sherry and I managed to draw blood from a back leg and sent the client on her way with the plasma, antibiotic eye drops, pain medicine, and specific instructions to recheck the following day. I was relieved that Dean was working the next day and could deal with her.

Not even an hour later, Dean called to tell me that Mrs. Beehive had seen him out mowing his lawn on her way home and had pulled into his driveway. She made Dean look at the eye, still numbed and stained. He agreed with my assessment and treatment and assured her I knew what I was doing.

"I'm sorry, Mel." he said, sympathetically. "I really don't go to the mental hospital and recruit clients. They just seem to find me."

The next day, Rocky had his recheck. Mrs. Beehive was all smiles when she came in and handed Rocky over to Dean without hesitating.

"The eye is much improved," Dean said. "There's some scar tissue coming in already."

As Dean handed Rocky back to her, the owner said: "Now, Rocky, you thank Dr. LeBeau. He saved your eye!"

Over time, Dean's clients accepted me. My own client list was growing, and we were consistently busy.

Life as a general practitioner was very different from emergency work. I could sleep at night and had weekends off. I had an appointment book and knew in advance what my cases were. Most important, I had a life outside of work. Things as simple as just being able to have dinner together every night and to enjoy our animal family in the evenings were real pleasures. My ER life had been hard on Steve, too. I vowed to make the next half of our lives more about our family and less about work.

Not only had my home life changed, but I noticed right away that even the clients at Elm Ridge were different. Most of the time, our clients were glad to see us. They were not upset, irate, or in an extreme state, as was common at the ER. Clients coming to an emergency clinic were not concerned about my years of experience. Despite my solemnly framed degrees, licenses, and awards on the wall, they did not immediately trust my skills.

I understood that clients have a bond with their family vet or doctor. When confronted by an unfamiliar doctor during a crisis, they were naturally distrustful. I did my best not to be insulted by ER clients' skepticism, knowing

I was much more experienced in dealing with emergencies than their family vet would ever be.

I missed the adrenaline rush of emergency work, the thrill of being presented with a critical case and having to pull out all the stops to diagnose and save the pet before it died. But the trade-off was worth it. At Elm Ridge, my clients knew me, trusted me. They even cared about me.

I cared about them, too. This was new to me. At Elm Ridge, my clients were becoming an extension of my own family. When their pets passed away, I grieved with them. Euthanasias were so much harder to deal with than they had been at the ER. Knowing the pet and the client made each euthanasia very personal and sad. When a client passed away, I grieved as if I had lost a family member. By the end of the first year in private practice, we had lost five members of our client family.

One of those was Mrs. Beehive. She had warmed up to all of us and was actually friendly. Although she always preferred to see Dean, she was no longer abrasive with the rest of us. We learned surprising things about her. Not only was she an accomplished, highly trained operatic soprano, but she was also a phenomenal home baker, a talent we came to appreciate. On a mission to pick up some flea medicine, she surprised us with a huge basket of delicious, homemade cookies. The next morning, we learned that only a few hours after we had seen her she had passed away suddenly from a ruptured appendix. Our entire staff felt the shock and loss as if we had lost a grandmother.

During the next two years, as our client family grew, we had to leave our tiny space and move to a larger facility down the road. In 2007, Stacy Bridges, who had worked for me at the emergency clinic, graduated from veterinary school. The plan was that she would join us and that Dean would gradually step away.

To meet the demand of our growing caseload, we added more assistants, techs, and receptionists. Elm Ridge was now a full-fledged practice.

Chapter 16

A Peaceable Kingdom

One more critter joined our family that summer of 2007. This one didn't take up much space at all, thank goodness, as bed real estate was at a premium. This latest addition was a brilliantly colored bird, a screaming eagle known as Screamie, who weighed all of five ounces.

I bought the sun conure from Morrison's, the local pet store, as a birthday present for Steve, who missed rehabilitating wild birds. Mrs. Morrison didn't sell wild birds. She hand-raised all her birds from the egg so that they would be particularly tame.

As soon as that little orange-and-yellow bird met Steve, she hopped onto his finger, walked up his arm, and perched on his shoulder. Screamie was in love. Dillie watched Screamie making herself comfortable and hissed. She was not pleased about sharing her daddy's affection. An adult now, Dillie stretched up her neck, grabbed Screamie by her green tail feathers, and threw her across the room.

Steve yelped and ran over to the fallen bird, who squawked and screeched. When he picked her up to make sure she was okay, the shaken bird retreated to the security of his shoulder.

"Oops!" Steve warned. "You had better watch out, Screamie."

That little bird turned out to be as fearless as her name-sake, our national bird. Steve stroked Dillie's cheek and said, "Now, Dillie, you have to be gentle with this bird." Screamie waddled slowly down his arm and bit Dillie square on the nose. Dillie shook her head from side to side, fluffed her tail, and stomped away. After that, Dillie let Screamie be.

When Spazz met Screamie and sniffed her to size her up, she did the same thing, chomping him right on the nose. Neffie had a similar run-in soon after. Though the cats were naturally curious about birds, and Spazz had certainly terrorized his share at the clinic, Screamie demonstrated that she was off-limits from the first moment. She even went after me if I got too close to Steve in her presence. She wanted to have him all to himself.

Everyone settled into a daily routine, which, of course, revolved around Dillie. She was the first up every morning, standing on the bed to lick Steve and me until we woke up at 5 a.m. sharp. Throughout our marriage, Steve and I had never owned an alarm clock, and we surely didn't need one now. Dillie's internal timekeeping mechanisms were more finely tuned than an atomic clock.

After Steve stumbled into the bathroom to take a shower, Dillie jumped off the bed. She followed Steve and head-butted the shower door. The banging got the cats out of bed and downstairs to sit by their dishes, patiently waiting for their favorite part of the morning. I got up next. Last was Lady, who always tried to grab a few extra minutes of sleep. Just as Steve and Dillie headed downstairs, she jumped up as if she had been awake the whole time and headed down with them.

Screamie slept downstairs in a large, unclosed cage. Resting in a little box inside the cage, she was quiet all night. As soon as she heard the procession coming down the steps, she started to squawk. When Steve's feet hit the last step, she flew to her place on his shoulder.

So began the day. One by one, the animals got fed. Neffie ate her meal and jumped up on top of the cupboards for a morning nap. The others went single file to the barn to tend to the horses and do the chores. Even Screamie went, hiding in Steve's warm Carhartt jacket and flannel shirt when it was cold, with just her little orange head peeking out at his chest. Dillie never entered the barn. She grazed along the fence line nearby, as Steve and the others greeted the horses with fresh hay and grain.

The horses looked forward to the morning routine. Even wicked Cammie toned down her mean streak as she waited for her daily meal. Kibbles took a long lick on Lady's back and tried to nuzzle Screamie. The towering, old Thoroughbred, a foot taller than Steve, was the one animal Screamie knew not to challenge. As Kibbles cast his shadow over Steve's shoulders, Screamie hunkered down inside her flannel nest.

After the horses were fed and watered, Dillie rejoined the group. Steve walked around the yard, checking the fences, picking up any branches that had fallen into the yard, and looking for frogs and mice in the pool. Dillie was always just a step or two behind. Occasionally, she stopped to eat a leaf or nibble a new shoot that had dared to grow on her favorite weep-no-more cherry tree. Distracted, she would look up, realize that Steve was more than a step away, and trot to catch up.

Dillie's playfulness was at its fullest at this time of day. She and Lady played hide-and-seek with Lady's toys, or Dillie ran around the yard at full speed on her own, her white tail fluffed up and switching like a pendulum. She expertly dodged trees and literally kicked up her heels as she gamboled around the yard.

Sometimes she and Steve played their favorite game, "Toro, Toro." Steve discovered that if he picked up the blue solar pool cover, Dillie would charge it like an enraged bull. He cut a corner off the cover just for her and wielded it like a matador's cape, shouting, "Toro! Toro!" Dillie would run through the pseudo cape, then pirouette, kicking triumphantly, and run away. Then she returned, head down like a bull, charging the other side of the cape. The game continued until Dillie lost interest and moved on to the next delicious flower.

When Dillie was finished with her game, Steve said, "Okay, guys, let's go see what Mom is up to."

All the animals and Steve returned to the house in single file: human with bird, cats, dog, and deer marching into the house just as I was walking out the door.

Steve gave Dillie a fresh bowl of ice. Ice was one of her favorite treats. She was adept at cracking the cubes with her back molars and had even learned to tip over glasses with her lips to spill out the cubes. Glass tumblers soon became extinct in the household and were replaced with plastic cups.

Dillie had learned a trick for when she couldn't find enough ice in glasses. On the refrigerator door was a large beige button. If she put her nose on the button, ice, that crunchy treat, came out with a clunk. When Steve had not put out enough ice in Dillie's bowl, she helped herself and got it fresh, right from the refrigerator door.

Like her wild cousins, Dillie was most active in the morning and at twilight, and slept most of the rest of the day, although she did not sleep on a muddy forest floor. She slept on a Sealy Posturepedic mattress, wrapped in 300-thread-count Egyptian cotton sheets and a Pendleton wool blanket. When her morning ritual was complete, Dillie climbed the stairs and headed back to bed. Without any humans to take up space, she sprawled out in Steve's spot, her head resting on his pillow.

Neffie would lie down next to her to enjoy the warmth of Dillie's large body. Emboldened, she stayed on top of the covers. Neffie did not have to hide as she did at night. Her nemesis, Lady, was wherever Steve was, and Spazz kept his distance from Neffie. If Spazz chose to take a catnap during daylight hours, he adjourned to his own room at the other end of the hallway. The afternoon sun streamed through the windows of his room, and if he positioned himself just so, he could bask in the sunbeam.

When Dillie got up in the afternoon to go downstairs and grab whatever snack Steve had left for her that morning, as well as to help herself to more ice from the refrigerator, she would pass by the open doorway of Spazz's room and stop to watch him sunning himself on the bed. Her satellite-dish ears would rotate for better reception as she listened to him purr. Then she headed down the steps. When she came back up to bed, she would stop in the doorway and watch Spazz again.

Eventually, Dillie's limitless curiosity drew her into the room. She flipped on the electric switches with her lips and turned the lights and ceiling fan off and on. She licked the doors and walls, tasting, sensing, exploring. She sniffed the air. Spazz's room overlooked the pool. With the window cracked open, the breeze was lush with the fragrance of what was left of the butterfly bushes, rose of Sharon, and cherry trees she nibbled on all the time. It must have been too appealing, and Dillie effortlessly leaped onto the bed.

Spazz allowed her to stay, as long as she tended to his grooming needs and didn't crowd him. Licking and grooming were allowed, nibbling on his ears was not. If Dillie tried, Spazz swatted her on her nose with just enough claw power to get her attention. A visit with Spazz became incorporated into Dillie's afternoon: two p.m., Spazz massage. After this appointment, Dillie rejoined Neffie on the other bed.

One day, Dillie chose Spazz's room as her new daytime napping space. Then Neffie joined her, staying right by her side as always. They slept at the head of the bed, across the pillows. Spazz, annoyed, was forced to the other end of the bed. Sometimes Lady jumped up and joined the crew. Neffie stood her ground as long as Dillie surrounded her. This room became the place where all the animals lounged in the afternoon.

I was amazed when I poked my head in the door one afternoon and saw two cats, a dog, and a deer, all napping in peace. A peaceable kingdom before my eyes.

Chapter 17

The Evil That Men Do

After a mild and brilliant fall, winter hit with a vengeance. It was bitter cold, with harsh winds, mountains of snow, and ice inches thick. Dillie and the other animal members of the family were sheltered from the extreme weather. Even the horses were protected from the hard winter in the barn. Steve put coats on them and built a windbreak in front of the barn. For animals in the wild or who were kept outside, it was a punishing year.

Steve put fresh hay and grain by the edge of the woods to help the wild deer through the brutal season. Every night at about five p.m., a herd of does came through to get their meal. From the dining room windows, we watched them as they broke into pairs, moving from hay pile to hay pile. Steve learned to spread the hay all over the front yard to prevent the does from battling over it with their front hooves. As long as each doe had her own hay pile to eat from, the deer peacefully took their share and returned to the woods.

From my work experience, I knew that humans were capable of being much crueler than any animal. Though most of my clients were loving pet owners and good stewards of creation, I had witnessed the handiwork of profoundly evil people—animal abuse. I had seen dogs starved to death, a basset hound stomped to death by an irate boyfriend, a cat set on fire by a group of teenagers, kittens whose eyes and mouths had been superglued shut, a toy poodle cooked alive in a microwave by a psychopathic ten-year-old boy.

If it wasn't for the kindness of animal lovers that I witnessed every day, exposure to the ugliness in some human hearts would have made me give up on the species. I was always willing to help people who tried to fight animal abuse. That terrible winter, I received a phone call from a nearby humane organization about an abandoned pet deer.

A Humane Society officer from a neighboring county had heard about Dillie from another veterinarian. She called to ask if she could place a neglected deer with us on a temporary basis. The deer's owner was wanted by the police for a drug issue. He had fled the state, abandoning a white doe and several other animals. Not only did the offender's parents refuse to care for the animals but they also would not allow anyone on their property. The animals were starving.

The officer explained that she had gone to court to get a judge's permission to enter the property to rescue the animals. After several weeks, the judge finally granted her access for three hours. She and several volunteers were going to the property the following day to load up all the animals and get out within the three-hour window. She had secured spots for the goats and horses but needed housing for the deer.

When I told Steve about the doe, he was all in.

"We've got that whole half barn I built for Dillie," he said. "The doe could move right in there."

Dillie had never put one hoof in the barn.

"I need to put a gate on that stall," Steve told me as he headed toward the door.

He was already thinking ahead, assuming this doe was going to become a permanent fixture in our lives.

"This one better not move inside," I said, only half joking, "or we're going to have to get a bigger bed."

The next day, we met the officer from the Humane Society and two volunteers in the neighboring county. The plan seemed simple enough: Steve and I were to follow them to the farm, and they would use bolt cutters to gain access. Once inside the fence, the agents would lead out the horses and goats, and we were to get the deer.

"Do you have a dart gun?" I asked.

"No," said the officer, "I thought we would catch her with this." She held up a conventional dog leash.

Steve and I exchanged a look. You cannot just put a leash around a deer's neck and expect it to follow like a cocker spaniel. Even Dillie, who was used to a collar, would not allow that.

"Good thing I brought the xylazine," I said to Steve. I had a feeling we would need to sedate the deer.

We followed the Humane Society pickup truck and

horse trailer through a maze of icy country roads for what seemed an eternity. Finally, the truck stopped at a gated, run-down farm surrounded by a six-foot-tall wire fence. The Humane Society officer pulled out bolt cutters, and we breached the gate.

"Why didn't they just do that weeks ago without the court order?" Steve asked, annoyed by all the red tape involved in trying to save the animals.

I went to the back of our SUV to grab my medical bag. Steve started to stride ahead with the rest of the group, but then turned back to the truck.

"Stay here," he instructed me. "I don't want you to see this."

"What do you mean?" I asked, "I have to."

"It's bad, it's really bad."

Animal after animal lay dead. Horses, goats, dogs in cages, even a caged raccoon—all dead, their emaciated bodies frozen. Fourteen of God's creatures had starved or frozen to death. The only animal alive on the farm was the unusual all-white deer.

Tears welled in my eyes. I had never witnessed cruelty on such a massive scale.

Steve threw down his ball cap and let loose a string of profanities. He raged against the owner of the property who had allowed this to happen, the parents who could have prevented the suffering, and the court system that had failed to save the suffering animals before their slow, brutal deaths.

The emaciated doe was housed in a small shed with access to an eight-by-eight-foot wire pen. She was understandably terrified. Tail fluffed, she ran back and forth between the shed and the pen, panting. Her color was different from that of a regular white-tailed deer. The lack of color gave her head a very goat-like appearance. She looked more like a cross between a goat and an alpaca than a deer.

About Dillie's size, the doe was skin and bones. Her survival was a miracle. Deer are known to be very efficient foragers, and this deer had managed to stay alive by eating dead wood and frozen weeds.

"Let's get this doe out of here, now," Steve directed. "Do you have the sedative ready?"

Steve talked to the doe and tried to calm her, but she was frantic. The deer ran back and forth trying to get away. She stopped, panting, for a moment, and then started running again. The only option was to corner, sedate, and carry her into the horse trailer.

The three volunteers and Steve chased her from the shed to the pen and back, trying to wedge her into a corner. Just when they thought she was contained and I approached with the syringe, the terrified animal leaped over our heads and ran. In her debilitated condition she couldn't avoid us for very long. She finally stayed in the corner just long enough for the syringe to hit its mark. Afterward, she continued to walk back and forth slowly. Eventually, she began to stumble. About ten minutes later, she was down.

The rest was easy. We dragged her onto some blankets we had brought and carried her into the horse trailer. We shut the doors and drove away from the house of horrors.

Time was short. The sedative would keep the doe

asleep for only an hour. While she slept, I looked at Steve and knew we were going to have another member of our family. She was still snoozing when we drove up our long gravel driveway.

Steve got out and secured the horses in their stalls. Then he opened the traffic gate to the corral, and the doe was brought into the half of the barn Dillie was supposed to have inhabited before she discovered Egyptian cotton made for a much more comfortable bed than straw. I gave the sleeping doe a reversal agent, and the bewildered animal staggered to her feet.

"We'll keep her here," Steve told the Humane Society officer. "If that's okay. We've been thinking Dillie could use a friend."

It was settled. I had even picked out a name: Caprice. I chose the name because she resembled a goat. The scientific name for a member of the goat family is *caprine*.

"I wonder if Dillie will even know what type of animal Caprice is," I said.

"She'll know, all right," Steve answered. "I just hope they get along."

I invited the cold, sad group of animal lovers to come in to meet Dillie before they went on their way. She greeted each one of them with a lick, delighting them after the nightmare at the farm.

"She'll definitely get a good home here," the officer observed.

"We'll see to that," Steve answered.

After the group left, Steve busied himself in the kitchen preparing a plate of fruit for Caprice. Hearing the knife against the chopping board was to Dillie what hearing a can opener was to a cat. She came trotting down the steps and started stealing the fruit Steve was chopping.

I cautioned, "You have to be careful what you feed Caprice. She has been eating nothing but scrub. Her body isn't used to high-sugar foods."

Steve rarely took my advice when it came to his own animals and plans.

"I am just going to give her a little," he said. "The horses can have the rest. I just want her to know that she has a home."

He gathered up the plate and headed for the door.

"Let's go, Dillie. Come meet your sister."

"Wait," I said, "We don't know what diseases this deer might have. We should keep them separated for a week, until we find out if she's carrying anything. At least wait until I have a chance to examine her."

Once again, Steve's paternal instincts prevailed.

"Dillie won't go in the barn anyway. If Caprice is strong enough, they can meet over the fence tomorrow."

As we headed out into the cold, I wondered how long it would take until Caprice joined our family on the bed.

Despite the prospect of food, Caprice remained very skittish when Steve entered her part of the barn. Steve sat on a hay bale, letting her get used to him and enticing her with apple wedges, the few, that is, that Kibbles and Cammie did not steal from him as they hung their heads over the partition. Kibbles pulled off Steve's ball cap and slurped his head with his long, thick horse tongue.

After a time, Steve mixed the few remaining wedges into the hay pile that Caprice was nibbling on. She tolerated Steve from a distance. When he approached, she ran to the other side of the stall, only returning to her hay after he retreated to his perch.

I left Steve sitting with Caprice for about a half hour before he secured the stall for the night. Dillie waited for him at the fence and walked with him back to the house. "You are going to have to help me, girl," he said, bending over her. "You are going to have to teach Caprice that we won't hurt her."

Dillie licked Steve's hand and cheek.

That night, as the menagerie claimed their places in the bed, Steve laid out his plans for the rehabilitation and taming of Caprice. Each day, he would bring the apples and bananas to her and sit with her while she ate them. Each day, he would get a little closer. Eventually, he thought, she would associate him with food and lose her fear.

He was worried about her. "She is so thin. She has no body fat. Do you think it's warm enough out in the barn for her? Maybe we should bed her in the garage. . . ."

"Oh no, not again," I scolded. "We cannot have another animal in this house. It's crazy enough as it is!"

"What do you mean, 'crazy'?" he asked earnestly.

Wedged between us as always, Dillie spread her cloven hooves, stretched out her long legs, and pushed me to the edge of the bed.

Chapter 18

Capricious Fortune

Steve began his approach to Caprice while I was at work the next day. At first, she lost her fear of him and was soon taking fruit right from his hands. Despite my cautionary advice, he decided it was time for Dillie and Caprice to meet, at least through the fence. He left the stall door open and let Caprice wander into the part of the corral he had partitioned off for Dillie.

As Caprice emerged that first time, Dillie was curious, but not afraid. She must have thought the movement was the horses. She fluffed up her tail, prepared to run. When she realized that the animal was no bigger than herself, she calmed down. Moments later, she and the strange, white, goat-like deer were standing nose to nose, separated by a wire fence. Despite their dissimilar appearance, they each knew immediately that they were of the same species.

The introduction went so well that Steve was ready to take the next bold step, allowing them to meet in the yard. He left the corral gate open. Caprice soon worked her way out of the corral to meet Dillie. Caprice didn't hesitate to enter the other yard. She made a beeline for Dillie and tried to mount her like a mating stallion.

Steve was shocked. So was Dillie, who bolted. Caprice followed. Anytime Dillie stopped, Caprice tried to mount her.

Stepping in to separate them, Steve noticed that Caprice had equipment that Dillie didn't, and no doe should. "Oh my God!" he exclaimed. "You're a buck!"

The Humane Society officer had identified Caprice as a doe. Since the deer had no antlers or antler buds, we had all assumed this was true. In the commotion of capturing and transporting the animal, none of us had actually examined the deer. In daylight, Steve could see clearly that where Dillie had an udder, Caprice had the essential male anatomy.

He hurried Dillie into the house. She seemed relieved to escape this pestering creature. Caprice stayed outside, nose pressed up against the full-length window of the back door. He was in love.

Steve called me at work. "We have a problem," he said.

Steve started nearly all his phone calls with this line. I braced for the news. What could it be now? Broken washer? Flat tire? House on fire?

"This deer, Caprice . . . ," he began, not quite knowing how to finish. "I know I'm not a vet or anything, but I do know male parts when I see them. And I saw them on this deer!"

"What?" I said in disbelief.

"We can't keep Caprice if he's a buck," Steve said. "You

have to come home and neuter him now. You have to take care of it right away."

My surgeries were done for the day, so I grabbed a surgery pack, suture, scrub, clippers, sterile gloves, an antibiotic injection, and a tetanus shot. I still had the sedative in my medical bag from yesterday. When I arrived home a few minutes later, my nephew Matt pulled in the driveway behind me. He and Steve were building a race car together, and Matt had stopped by to do some welding. Matt was accustomed to his slightly crazy Aunt Melanie and his very crazy Uncle Steve. He was not a bit fazed when I greeted him with a strange rhyme: "Glad you are here, you can help me castrate this deer."

Steve had corralled Caprice, whom he'd renamed Gorgeous George. I led Steve and Matt to the barn, our default surgical suite. I did not want to have to transport the deer sedated to and from the clinic to do the procedure. Since I wasn't planning to remove the abdominal testicle, the barn would be fine.

I sedated George and waited for him to lie down.

"I can't believe he doesn't have any antlers," Steve said.

"He wouldn't have antlers this time of year," I replied.

"Yeah," Steve said, "but he should at least have antler buttons. There should be something there. I petted his head—there isn't anything."

"Are you sure he's male?" Matt asked innocently.

Steve bristled. "I'm sure. I saw what I saw."

We would know soon enough. George had just started to fold his legs underneath him.

Once the deer was down, the explanation was obvious. Steve had indeed seen what he thought he saw. George was male, but he had only one visible testicle. He was cryptorchid. The other testicle had not descended from his abdomen. Since the abdominal testicle could not produce testosterone, George didn't have sufficient male hormone to grow antlers, but he did have enough from his normal testicle to take one look at Dillie and make his move.

I hadn't done surgery in a barn since my vet school days. I tried to make the incision sterile by clipping and scrubbing it and using sterile instruments. I gave Gorgeous George the antibiotic and tetanus injections, intended to ward off any infection from a bed of straw, a less-than-ideal surgery table.

"Have you ever castrated a deer before?" Matt asked.

"Nope," I replied. "But the anatomy is pretty much the same no matter the species."

The plan was to remove only the outer testicle. The one in the abdomen would have to stay. The sedative would not be a strong enough anesthetic for an abdominal surgery, nor was our dusty barn the place for it. Without his only viable testicle, George would be rendered sterile.

Both men grimaced as I made the necessary incision and ligations.

"That was fast," Matt said.

"It's a skill every girl should learn. It keeps our husbands in line."

Steve squirmed. "I'll sleep with one eye open for the rest of my life."

"You'd better."

Surgery done, I grabbed my stethoscope and did a thorough physical exam on George. After I injected the penicillin and tetanus antitoxin, I reversed his sedation.

George was up on his hooves in minutes.

"Do you think this will stop him from chasing Dillie around?" Steve asked.

"I don't know," I said. "He's still a male, and he still may be interested in her, even if he can't do much about it."

"Dillie was really upset by him chasing her. We'll have to keep them apart for a while."

"This was only supposed to be a temporary placement anyway," I reminded Steve. "Maybe the Humane Society will come up with another home."

As we walked back to the house, I announced, "I'm going to head out to the farm supply store. I only had a little tetanus antitoxin at the office. I need to get some more."

Tetanus was rare in dogs and almost unheard of in cats, so the clinic stocked only a small supply of the antitoxin. But deer, like their sheep and goat cousins, were very susceptible to tetanus. Having surgery in a barn greatly increased George's risk of developing this deadly bacterial disease.

I left the boys tinkering in the garage and headed out.

At the farm store, I selected the items I needed and a few treats for the horses, Dillie, and Lady. The only other customer was a man at the counter with a single bag of horse grain. He was taking a very long time, asking the clerk about the feed's yield in painfully specific terms. The sale finally took place, and the horse owner shoved his change in his pocket and headed out the door.

Relieved to see him go, the young clerk shook his head, and said to me, "Sorry about that."

"That's okay," I answered. "I'm a vet. I have clients like that, too."

The clerk smiled. He was a tall, thin teenager, with bright red hair and pale blue eyes. He looked at my anti-toxin purchase. "Can't you order this yourself?"

"Yes, but I need it today." I told him about rescuing George thinking he was a doe, and how he had chased Dillie around the yard. I explained I had had to neuter him right away.

"My dad has a deer farm, all does," the clerk said. "He collects their urine to make hunting lures. He's been looking to get a buck to let him know which ones are in heat, but the buck has to be castrated so he won't be dangerous. Do you think you'd be willing to sell this guy?"

I couldn't be sure, but I thought I heard a chorus of angels singing "Hallelujah." There are times in life when God puts people together at just the right time and place.

"We couldn't sell him to you, but we would be happy to give him to you," I answered. "I just have to check with my husband and the Humane Society that placed him with us, but that would be great."

Two days later, the clerk and his father came to pick up George. They were so experienced with deer that they didn't even need to sedate him. They loaded him into a special crate they had built to transport their does, and farm-strong as they both were, hoisted the crate onto the bed of their pickup truck.

"Talk about capricious fortune," I said to Steve, as George headed off to his new home. "In less than a week, he went from being the only animal alive on the entire farm, nearly starving to death, to being the only male among a harem of does."

"Poor thing," Steve answered, with a twinkle in his eye. "Not sure which is worse."

Chapter 19

A Thief in the Night

Kibbles and Cammie left us at the end of that harsh winter. Having completed her studies, Catherine was moving to Arizona with her horses. Steve said tearful good-byes. He loved those guys and was going to miss them, despite having had to carry water out to the barn twice a day during the frigid winter.

"Maybe it is time we downsize a little," he said, trying to make the best of a sad situation.

After Kibbles and Cammie had gone, Steve didn't go into the barn for nearly a month. When he did, Dillie followed right behind, her first time in the barn.

"This is where you were supposed to stay, Dillie," Steve informed her. "Not as nice as our bedroom, huh?"

Although Steve and the animals no longer visited the

horses on their daily march, they sometimes encountered wild does outside the fence. When they did, Dillie fluffed up her tail and raced right to Steve's side. The does watched her with intense interest.

Dillie was already spending much of her day in Spazz's room and soon began sleeping there, too. She stood on the bed, stretched her neck, and pulled the chain of the ceiling fan. She liked the breeze.

"I kind of miss her on the bed," Steve said one night.

"I don't," I answered, stretching out my legs. There was a lot more room without sharing our bed with a fully grown deer.

Dillie still visited us many nights, turning on the lights with her lips as she walked into the room. She never turned them off. One very groggy human had to get out of bed to do that. We realized that she did this purposefully. Her poor vision made it difficult for her to see even shapes in low light.

She stood next to her beloved Papa, placed her head on his chest, and gazed at him with loving eyes. As Steve stroked her face, she licked his hand, her tongue flipping out the side of her mouth. She eventually returned to her new room. Only rarely did she jump onto our bed. She was a big girl now.

Every now and then, she came into our room in the middle of the night and woke us up with her mischief. One night she pulled down the curtains and rod with a loud crash. Almost every night she went into the bathroom and opened drawers and cupboards to look for interesting things. Toothpaste was her favorite target. If the tube was left anywhere within reach of her long neck, it was destroyed.

Once we awoke to the sounds of things falling into the bathtub. When we investigated, we found Dillie standing in the tub having a bubble bath, shampoo and soap bottles around her, the faucet on full blast. She often head-butted the shower or cupboard doors, rubbing her nonexistent antler buds. "Dillie's playing the drums again," Steve would mutter when the noise woke us.

Her nightly routine also included visits to the kitchen. She deftly used her lips to open cupboard and pantry doors in search of snacks. Steve always left out a tray of fruits and salads and a big box of fresh timothy hay for her, but she preferred a treasure hunt. Finally, Steve cleared out a cupboard and stashed granola bars there just for this purpose.

I decided to film Dillie's nightly cupboard raid with a trail camera I had won at an auction. These cameras are usually set up by hunters to monitor deer and other animals as they move past the camera in the woods. Dillie was a deer of a different lifestyle, but still a deer, and the camera worked perfectly.

I set it up one night and went to bed. The next morning I had a good laugh. Like a thief, she snuck into the kitchen and looked around nervously. She tossed her head up in the air and licked the refrigerator door. Certain the coast was clear, she stepped toward her target, the cupboard. She opened its door, using her lips and nose with the dexterity of a safecracker, and retrieved the tasty loot.

The next frames of the video showed her chewing a granola bar, wrapper and all, sliding it back and forth in her mouth like a kid eating corn on the cob. She continued doing this for nearly a minute, then dropped the empty wrapper and returned to the cupboard for another treat.

Dillie's natural curiosity, incredible sense of smell, giraffe-like reach, and dexterous lips were always getting her in trouble. One night, an especially noisy *crash! bang! boom!* from downstairs woke us.

Steve found Dillie standing in the living room amid the shattered remains of his cigar humidor. She was nibbling on some ten-dollar cigars. Steve kept the humidor on top of an eight-foot cabinet, which he thought was safely out of Dillie's reach. He had underestimated the problem-solving ability of our determined deer. She had climbed onto the sofa next to the cabinet and pulled the humidor down. She had her choice of cigars, but preferred the Lot 123 Perdomos and the Cusanos—the most expensive of the bunch.

"Well, you have very good taste, Dillie," Steve said as he salvaged what remained of his collection. "No wasting time on the cheap ones, huh?"

From that day on, the cigars were stored in the "Dillie-proof" room. I had been using this small room as a downstairs office. When the door was closed, Dillie could not get in. The room soon became the only place in the house in which cigars, houseplants, and vases of flowers were safe from the prying tongue and agile lips of a most accomplished cervid thief. I grew hibiscus plants in the makeshift vault and treated Dillie to succulent blossoms every day. I thought the plants would be safe there, but one day I spotted Dillie trying to turn the doorknob with her lock-pick lips.

"Oh, no, you don't!" I scolded, chasing her away. "You are not getting in there!"

Once again, she proved she was not to be denied when she was determined. Coming home one afternoon, I found the door of the Dillie-proof room open and the contents ransacked. She had been busy. The cigars had survived, but only because Dillie had spent her time chewing every leaf from the five hibiscus plants.

"Who needs napalm?" I said when I showed Steve the bare branches of the plants. "The army should just deploy a herd of deer. They can defoliate a jungle in seconds, and there are no nasty side effects."

Like an exasperated Ricky Ricardo calling for Lucy, Steve shook his head and shouted, "Dilllllliiiieeeee!"

Chapter 20

Summer Surprise

The summer day was set on broil. Dean asked me if his two young grandchildren could spend a day playing in our pool. The little boy and girl had traveled from Washington State to visit their "Grandpa Buckeye," as they called him, because of his Ohio State obsession. The children were hot and bored, and Dean had run out of ways to entertain them. Always delighted to see Dean, who adored his grandkids, I made a frosty pitcher of lemonade to cool us off.

Dillie was up in bed when Dean and the kids arrived. The sound of children playing drew her to her window, which overlooked the pool. Children meant fun and treats.

Dean's seven-year-old granddaughter decided just then that she needed to use the potty. As the little towhead sat on the commode in the downstairs bathroom, Dillie pushed the door open with her nose.

Seconds later, one very frightened, wide-eyed child came running outside, bathing suit bottom around her ankles.

"Grandpa!" she screamed. "There's . . . there's . . . there's something in there!"

Dillie followed behind her, ready to play.

Grandpa Buckeye grinned and picked up his granddaughter. He told his grandchildren Dillie's story and introductions were made.

Dean's grandson was a curious boy of ten. "Is Dillie chewing gum?" he asked after watching Dillie up close for a while.

"I'll let your grandfather answer that question," I said. "He's the expert."

Dean explained to his grandkids that deer, like cows, have stomachs with separate rooms or chambers to help them digest a wide variety of plants.

"Deer eat everything—flowers, fruit, grass, vegetables, and some tougher things like pine needles and even bark. It's all delicious to them. They eat the available food until they stuff the first chamber of their stomach where the food is stored."

He went on to describe how Dillie would bring the stored food back into her mouth to chew it thoroughly, which turned the food into cud. She would then swallow the chewed food, which went to the second chamber, where it was broken down even further in a process called fermentation. As the food broke down, it would release methane gas that could make her burp if she ate too many sweets.

"Just like us when we eat too much junk food!" the bright boy said.

Dean wrapped up his lesson, saying, "Dillie chews the food again, and it passes into the third room, where water is added, and then on to the last room, where acid finishes digesting the food so that it can be absorbed from her intestines to nourish her body."

"She sure does a lot of chewing. Deer have to work hard to eat."

Dean laughed and tousled his grandson's hair.

The kids had a great time splashing with Dillie in the summer sun. The surprising playmate made their day. They couldn't believe that they had made friends with a deer.

Chapter 21

Musical Deer Repellent

Maintaining a household with so many pets can be exhausting. Steve and I needed a break now and then. We wanted to visit friends in Florida, go on a blues cruise, and spend time with Steve's family in Oregon. Carol Zeh to the rescue again! Zeh and our animal family got along well. She had bonded with Dillie since fawnhood, Lady followed her everywhere, and Spazz and Neffie curled up on the couch with her at night. Screamie the bird was another story: She allowed Zeh to feed her, but not to hold her—no one could replace her beloved Papa.

A vigorous amateur musician, Zeh appeared the day we left with her sleeping bag, trombone, guitar, banjo, several baskets of laundry, and a week's supply of vegetarian food. Zeh has been a vegetarian for more than thirty years. Her meals were interchangeable with Dillie's.

"How do you know whose is whose?" I quipped, looking at her provisions for the week.

"Dillie's is on the bigger tray, and she gets the more expensive lettuce," Zeh said. "We'll share the linguine, but the timothy hay is all hers."

Whenever we went away, Steve left a fifteen-to-twenty-page book of detailed instructions about Dillie on the kitchen counter. He called Zeh at least ten times a day.

The conversations went like this. "How's Dill?" Steve would ask. Zeh replied, "She found Mel's Elton John Songbook in the piano room. She just finished 'Candle in the Wind' and now she's on to 'Goodbye Yellow Brick Road.'"

"She's playing the piano?" Steve asked in disbelief.

"No, she's eating the music," Zeh said. "Now she's chewing her cud in three-four time."

One evening, Zeh, Lady, and Dillie were all lying on Dillie's blanket on the living room floor, watching *Apollo 13* and sharing popcorn and granola bars. After Dillie went up to bed, Zeh turned off the movie and decided to practice her trombone. Just as she played the first few bars, she heard Dillie jump off her bed. The thud was unusually loud and pronounced. Bounding down the steps, Dillie made a left turn at the banister, her eyes wide, ears flattened, tail fluffed and twitching, and hackles standing straight up.

"What's the matter, Dillie?" Zeh asked. "You don't like Sousa?"

Zeh tried a calmer tune, but had only finished six bars

when Dillie began to snort and paw the carpet with her sharp hooves. Then Dillie charged into the living room and ran in circles.

Zeh had never seen Dillie act this way. *Mad deer! Mad deer!* she thought as she put the trombone away and went to the living room to soothe Dillie.

"Dillie," Zeh said, "do I play that badly? Don't worry, you'll never have to come to any of my concerts."

Dillie eventually calmed down. Zeh was just learning the trombone, and apparently her playing sounded like a raging bull moose. Zeh concluded she needed more lessons.

While we were away, Zeh switched to the string instruments—guitar and banjo—she had been playing for years. Dillie loved music. Any time I'd play Pavarotti or Josh Groban while sitting at my computer, Dillie would come into my office to rest her head on my desk. Zeh's guitar soothed Dillie, who chewed her cud while Zeh played.

Chapter 22

Howie's Hideaway

Living in the woods made us accustomed to wild visitors in our yard. Raccoons and opossums raided the bird feeder every night, causing Lady to spend hours with her nose pressed against the plate-glass door, eager to chase them away. Wild deer came through the yard every day. Bunnies, skunks, foxes, beavers, wild turkeys, and even coyotes were frequent drop-ins.

Dillie lived behind an eight-foot-tall fence, as required by Ohio law. She was not allowed to mingle with wild deer, nor were they allowed to come inside, supposedly for her protection. This barrier also prevented predators like coyotes and stray dogs from endangering her.

Dillie showed a natural curiosity about the small, peaceful wild animals that made it through the fence. She chased them around the yard without fear. A nesting pair of mallards, who used the pool cover as their private pond each spring, were such routine visitors that they no longer scooted away from Dillie. She started nuzzling them as if they were her familiar cats. In the early evening, the cottontail rabbits grazed right next to her. She paid them no attention, content to share her space with any unthreatening animal.

The summer Dillie turned six, she met an unexpected visitor who captured her attention.

We had bought Dillie a baby pool to avoid crashing into her while we swam laps. One day, while she was enjoying a splash in her kiddie pool as I swam in the main pool, I noticed that she was staring at something near the garage. Her hair stood straight up. She stomped a hoof.

"What's wrong with you, Dillie?" I called from the pool.

Dillie froze, all four hooves in her baby pool, tail fluffed up.

Steve appeared at the back door. He looked in the same direction as Dillie. "What's that goat doing here?" he asked.

"What?" I answered, thinking I had heard him wrong. "What do you mean?"

"There's a goat over there," he said, pointing toward the garage. "A big white goat. With horns. Inside the fence."

I followed his finger but couldn't see what Steve and Dillie were looking at. "You're crazy," I said. "How would a goat get through the fence? It's eight feet tall!"

"There's a goat—right there." Steve pointed again. "It has horns that curl around its head and a long white beard. It's big."

"Oh, come on," I said, splashing water at him.

"No, really! There *is* a goat right there. Look at Dillie," he said, gesturing at her. "She sees it."

"Okay, okay, "I said. "I'll get out of the pool. But you'd better not be messing with me."

I swam back from the deep end and climbed out of the pool.

"He just left," Steve said.

"I knew you were pranking me." I didn't believe a word he was saying.

Steve was adamant. "There was a goat, I swear."

"Then what happened to it? Where is it? Did it fly back over that huge fence?" I wasn't falling for another one of his jokes.

"He didn't climb over the fence. He crawled under it."

"Oh, right." I rolled my eyes and got back in the water to finish my laps.

Steve had a well-earned reputation as a super prankster. Once he even planted a tree in the middle of a friend's driveway—an elaborate gag involving a concrete saw, construction cones, a wheelbarrow, a shovel, a bag of quick-drying concrete, and a six-foot cherry tree. Steve's friend Ray made the mistake of telling Chevy-man Steve that his Ford truck was better. Steve was quick to say that the only thing Fords were good for was giving Chevys something to tow. Ray told him he was full of BS. Steve repaid him by running a classified ad in the local newspaper with Ray's telephone number, offering "free bull manure, by the truckful." Ray was inundated with callers asking if they could come by to get their free truckful of bull dung.

Fully aware of the effort Steve would put into a prank, I was not about to fall for the goat story. I had no doubt that he would buy a goat and hire a helicopter to hoist it over the fence if it would convince me that the goat was real. Even after my nephew Kyle came over to swim that day and asked, "Why is there a goat in your driveway?" I remained convinced that Steve had put him up to it.

During the next six days, every time we sat down for dinner, Steve said, "I saw that goat again."

"Right," I said. "That goat must have special powers. He can disappear at will."

On the seventh day, I was sitting on our wide front porch, reading a book and enjoying the warm summer day, with Lady right by my feet. Dillie was on the porch as well, licking Lady and trying to steal ice cubes from my iced tea, when she came to white-fluffed attention. Lady stood up and growled, wagging her black pom-pom tail with the same excitement as when a squirrel came into view. I looked up. On the front walk, six feet away, was a goat. A big, white goat with horns that curled around its ears.

I called Steve, who was tinkering in the garage. "Steve, that goat is here, on the front sidewalk!"

He couldn't resist. "What goat?"

The goat wasn't healthy. His coat was ratty, and he had weeping sores on his sides. His wrists, knees, and ankles were swollen, and he limped on his back left leg when he walked. The horns curled around his ears in such a tight spiral that they were cutting into them. He was downright filthy from his little tail to his wattles. Every bit a he, his prominent male package was in full display.

I called out to him. "Hey, goatie goat! Are you hungry?"

He looked up, his horizontal pupils focusing on me, then leaped in alarm and sprinted toward the garage.

Steve called, "I just saw him go under the garage. That's where he's living."

Lady leading the way, I walked down to the garage. Steve pointed out the goat's suite. Underneath one side of the garage was a three-foot crawl space, which had become the luxury accommodation of one very homely goat. Lady sniffed around, peeked underneath the building, and growled.

"He's way under there," Steve said. "Now will you apologize for calling me crazy?"

"No way," I answered. "You are crazy. You just happened to be right about this goat."

I peered into the crawl space and saw brown eyes looking back. "Only we could have a goat show up in our yard," I said.

The goat looked as if he'd been feral forever. He could be carrying parasites and diseases. I didn't want him near Dillie. Fortunately, the garage was outside the fence, and Dillie didn't have access to that part of the yard.

"If he gets within thirty feet of her, I will chase him away," Steve said. "If he keeps trying, maybe we'll have a goat barbecue."

Steve and Lady went to get room service for our new guest. Steve placed hay, sliced apples, and water at the edge of the crawl space, then stood back and watched the hungry goat poke his nose out, take an apple slice, and retreat into his hideaway.

"I never saw such an antisocial goat," I said. Usually, goats were gregarious, friendly creatures, but this guy was terrified of people. "He's a complete recluse, like Howard Hughes."

"Hey, Howie," Steve called as he pushed the food tray farther under the garage. "Come get your room service. Don't worry, there aren't any germs!"

Dillie was still anxious, puffed up and pawing at the ground to intimidate the cowardly goat.

During the next few days, Howie became a little more adventurous. He came out to eat his food, even when we were watching. If anyone tried to approach him, he would dart back to his sanctuary under the garage.

The goat became part of our daily routine. Dillie grew more accustomed to seeing him and didn't react defensively when he joined her at a respectful distance. Lady stopped growling when he was near.

But Howie still wouldn't allow us to touch him. I desperately wanted to start antibiotics, wormers, and lice treatment. Since the complex goat digestive system inactivates most oral medicines, the best way to treat him would be with injectable and pour-on medications. But Howie was a long way from letting us get close enough to treat him. Oral antibiotics seemed my only option. I hid a tablet within an apple on his food tray. He was too wily for that. He ate all the grain, berries, and greens. The only thing left was a delicious-looking, bright green Granny Smith apple with a sulfa drug hidden in its center.

"Funny that he knows there's something in there," I remarked. "He's like a giant cat." Most dogs take medicine easily if mixed with a little peanut butter or cheese, but fooling a cat is nearly impossible. A pet owner could put out an entire buffet of tuna, chicken, and cat food to hide one drop of antibiotics within a morsel of the feline's favorite food. The cat would run to the buffet, take one whiff, and turn away in a huff. Howie seemed to have the same ability. No matter where I tried to hide his tablet, it would be the only food item he left behind.

After two more weeks of spoiling Howie with crispy, fresh salads, fresh hay, and sweets, he allowed me to get close enough that I was able to apply a wormer to his back. He would need to be restrained for me to give him an injection.

Steve decided to set a trap for Howie, so we could at least move him into the barn. He had his own reasons for wanting to catch the goat. An intact male goat has the unpleasant odor of a skunk. The fumes wafting up from Howie's hideaway were polluting Steve's garage time. He and his buddies, whom I called the Garage Rats, devised what they considered a brilliant plan. They were going to set up left-over "fencing" from Dillie's pen in the corral. The fencing was actually a six-foot-tall dog cage with a gate. Steve and his buddies thought that if they could lure Howie from his hideaway into the pen with some treats, they could run up and close the door with Howie safely inside.

Their first attempt seemed promising. The guys set up the pen next to the entrance to Howie's suite under the garage and put the treats inside. Howie was no longer the starving waif he had been. His belly was always full, and he had no urgent need to risk getting more treats in the pen.

Steve instructed everyone to give Howie food, water, or treats only in the pen. Howie completely ignored the smorgasbord during the day. He feasted at night when no one was around to trap him. By morning, all the food was gone.

Steve was undaunted. "It's just a matter of time," he said. "Sooner or later he is going to go in that pen while I'm around, and I will get him."

A few days later, Howie ventured into the pen and started to nibble the hay and grain. Steve ran out of the garage and tried to close the door, but Howie saw him coming and rocketed out of the pen and back under the garage before Steve even reached the gate.

The Garage Rats regrouped. The new plan was to tie a rope on the gate and pull it shut remotely so that Howie would not have time to run out. They set his meal in the pen. They tested the rope pull, and it actually worked. Not only did the gate swing shut, but the latch caught. They were sure they would catch him now.

Within a few hours, the Garage Rats saw Howie enter the pen. Steve pulled the rope and heard the gate clang shut. The guys came running out to meet their quarry face-to-face. But it wasn't Howie's face that greeted them. They arrived at the pen just in time to see Howie's rear end scurrying under the fence, back to his bunker. He had escaped the pen the same way he had gotten into our yard in the first place.

In the end, it was not human inventiveness that would catch the crafty old goat, but lust. The next day, Howie was in the yard with Dillie, acting unusually friendly. He kept trying to approach her as a mate. Dillie refused to tolerate

Howie's advances. After scampering away from him several times, she ran into the house. If I hadn't closed the door behind her, the confused, lovesick goat might have followed her right into the kitchen. Howie peered longingly through the back door's full-length window.

"Now we have to catch him," I told Steve. "We're going to have to knock him out and neuter him as soon as possible. We can't have him chasing Dillie around like that."

Howie himself made other plans. At ten o'clock that night, I received a phone call from Sean, a friend who lived about a half mile from us through the woods. Sean had three female goats penned behind his house.

"Hey, Mel," Sean began, "did you and Steve put that goat in my pen?" I had run into Sean a few weeks ago and told him about Howard Hughes, the goat recluse.

"Put him in your pen? We can't even get near that goat."

"Well, he's in there, chasing my does around."

"Yeah, he's pretty horny, excuse the pun," I said.

"If I can get him in a stall, do you think you can come over tomorrow and knock him out and neuter him?" Sean's house was right behind my clinic "If you can do that," Sean continued, "I'll keep him."

"He's pretty sickly," I warned.

"I'll get him back in shape," Sean promised.

We completed our plan the next morning, and the newly neutered Howie moved to Sean's place. He's still there today, in a proper pen instead of a hollow under our garage.

Chapter 23

Bless the Beasts and the Children

Dillie, who followed Lady in everything, looked forward to visits from strangers and the neighborhood kids, who usually brought treats, such as licorice or flowers. Lady always gave visitors one of her toys, and then waited for the toy back or a treat of her own. Dillie, Lady, and the kids played in the backyard, supervised by Steve. The happy deer bucked and kicked her hooves high into the air as Lady scrambled around the yard. The children giggled in delight.

Strangers who rang our bell were rarely prepared to be greeted by Dillie. Many a mail carrier, UPS, delivery, or cable person was stunned to see a 150-pound white-tailed doe standing in the doorway or the kitchen.

A startled air-conditioner repairman sought me out in another room of the house one morning.

"Do you know there's a full-grown deer in your kitchen?" he asked.

"Is she eating bagels?" I had heard Dillie getting into the fresh bagels Steve had stashed in her cupboard for her morning treat.

The bewildered repairman grabbed his camera phone and sent a picture to his wife.

Dillie also had an encounter with the law. Steve was burning straw from the barn, which is illegal in Ohio. Dillie was inside with me. A firefighter saw the smoke and drove up our long driveway to investigate. When I answered the door, Dillie stuck her head out. The firefighter was wide-eyed.

"That's our deerhound, Dillie," I said.

The fireman was too busy writing a citation to respond. He handed me the slip then headed back to his truck without saying a word.

Dillie loved children. Summer meant the neighborhood kids were out of school, and they visited every day, riding up the driveway on their bikes. Dillie greeted them with licks and kisses. Sometimes the kids came over to swim. Dillie rarely swam laps anymore, unless she accidentally fell into the pool. She did like to wade down the steps and soak her hooves in the cool water or splash around in her plastic baby pool while the kids swam in the big pool.

There was one child Dillie did not like, one and only one: Steve's grandson Akheem. The relationship started friendly enough. Akheem had come that summer to spend a few weeks with Grandpa Steve. At nine years old, the boy was already very tall, athletic, and brimming with energy. He was constantly on the move. He loved to swim and could spend as much as twelve hours a day in the pool, until one of us would finally have to tell him it was time for bed.

At first, Dillie seemed happy to see him. She would stand in her baby pool and play with the hose while Akheem swam or practiced diving off the board. Usually, the local kids would join him in the pool, but their energy level was no match for his. After a few hours, they were ready to go back to their homes, leaving Akheem in the pool with no playmates except Dillie.

Akheem directed his energy at Dillie and started a game of tag. He ran out of the pool, slapped her gently on the backside, and then ran back into the pool, over and over again.

Dillie was not amused. She started to charge him, as if she were playing "Toro, Toro" with Steve, only seriously. She lowered her head, flattened her ears, and head-butted Akheem right back into the deep end—repeatedly. Eventually, every time Akheem approached the pool edge, she charged.

To a young boy, this was a fun game. To a deer, it was not. Dillie saw him as a threat. She was not charging to entertain but to eliminate.

Dillie didn't trust Akheem any more in the house than she did in the pool. During his visit, Dillie started to sleep with us again. One night, Akheem entered our bedroom to ask for an additional pillow. Dillie stood up in alarm and leaped off the bed. Tail fluffed and switching, she charged at Akheem, who scurried back to his room.

After Dillie's aversion to Akheem, we were worried that she would show aggression toward other children. The day after Akheem flew back to Oregon, the neighborhood boys were swimming in the pool, and Dillie was playing on her own in the yard. If a child stood on the pool edge, she would chase him back in, but without the ferocity Akheem had stirred in her.

Chapter 24

Video Victory

A year later, Akheem returned for a summer visit. He had grown a foot since his last visit, and even Steve, his own grandfather, had trouble recognizing him. Dillie didn't, though. When he walked into the house, Dillie took one look, flattened her ears, and immediately charged as if someone had played a cavalry bugle.

Akheem's second visit became a life-changing event for our little family. Although he was older and a little more mature, he was still a boy. Boys do things they are told not to do—like leave the gate to the yard open.

Fortunately, the major consequence of Akheem's mistake was the destruction of flowers and plants, which were off-limits to Dillie and her deforestation powers. But I started to worry. What if it happened again? What if a delivery person or one of the neighborhood kids left the gate open and we didn't discover the error until Dillie was loose? According to Ohio law, if a domestic deer wandered freely for more than a day, it had to be destroyed. The various restrictions were put into law with the intent of protecting domestic deer from contracting chronic wasting disease from wild deer. We do not know how the disease is transmitted or even what causes it, but the state has decided to err on the side of caution in prevention.

I wanted to find a way to track Dillie's whereabouts in case of the unthinkable.

"What we need," I told Steve, "is a GPS device, a LoJack for animals."

Steve was skeptical.

I researched several available devices, collar-worn GPS locators for dogs. Most of them were in the $300 to $400 range. Steve would never go for that. I settled on a similar, less expensive device.

Steve still grumbled about the price and the monthly fee.

"That gate has been left open only that one time," he complained, "We don't need to spend any money on this."

I was determined. The thought of searching through the woods for Dillie before animal control had to put her down terrified me.

Steve criticized the device from the day it arrived. Even when I demonstrated how I could go to my laptop and pull up a satellite image of the yard showing Dillie's location as a moving pin, he refused to be impressed by the technology. As he walked away, I noticed a banner ad on the GPS website. They were having a contest: "Submit a video on how you use your GPS, and you could win $1,000 and free service for life!"

The deadline was eight a.m. the next morning. Since it was a Sunday, I had the whole day to put the video together. I grabbed my camcorder and headed out to film Dillie nosing around the yard, eating a houseplant, and jumping on her bed.

I combed through the hundreds of images I had of Dillie and started to build the film clip. I downloaded the footage I had shot that afternoon. Everything had to be trimmed, tweaked, and timed. The video could be only a minute long. After four hours of editing, all that remained was to add the transitions between the edited clips and titles. Right then, my laptop died, just gave up the ghost without warning. All my work was lost.

There wasn't enough time to go down to the office to use a computer there. The day was almost over.

"Oh, what's the use?" I was ready to give up. "I probably wouldn't win anyway."

Just then, Steve appeared in the doorway with a box.

"UPS left this at the bottom of the driveway yesterday," he said looking down at the return address. "What have you done now?"

I had completely forgotten that I had ordered a replacement computer for the office. What serendipity!

"Give me that box!" I barked, grabbing it from him, and disappeared into my office.

The box was a sign—a sign that I was supposed to be victorious and make Steve appreciate technology. I was more determined than ever to win this contest

I had enough pieces and parts from old computers—keyboards, mouse, and monitors—to get the new computer up and running. When we sold the emergency clinic, all the computers at the clinic had come to my house to live out their days. They spent their retirement in the basement, which Steve called "the boneyard."

After dinner, I discovered I didn't have the right connector cable. I tore through the house. The last place I checked was a box of odds and ends I had picked up at a going-out-of-business sale at a local electronics store. Miraculously, I found a FireWire I to FireWire II cable.

I was back in business. The editing went faster the second time around, and all I had to do was submit the finished video. I decided to do that in the morning so I could give myself one last chance to tweak the final product.

Steve had already been in bed for several hours when I finally came upstairs for the night. Dillie was standing there as usual, licking Steve's face and wearing her GPS collar. The little green light flashed in the dark.

"I finally got the video done," I said with fake nonchalance. "I am going to win that contest, and when I do, you can no longer say anything bad about my computers."

I awoke that morning at six a.m. to discover that the power was out in the whole neighborhood. Fortunately, I had made a backup this time, so if necessary, I could take the file to the office and submit it from there. I got ready for work by candlelight. Just as I reached for my car keys, the power came back on. I ran downstairs, booted up my computer, and prayed as the video uploaded to the contest site.

That afternoon, Steve picked me up at the office for

lunch. As we pulled into the parking lot of the local diner, my cell phone rang. It was a representative from the GPS company's marketing agency.

"You won," he said, "hands down. We all watched the video over and over again. Does she really sleep in a bed?"

I slapped Steve on the shoulder and mouthed, "I won! Told you!"

The man explained that he would send a press release declaring Dillie the winner of the contest along with the video to the news networks in about a month.

"After that," he warned, "things might get a little crazy."

"Oh, we're used to crazy," I replied.

Chapter 25

Love at First Lick

Dillie-mania began.

After the press release went out, the first to call was Dawn Kendrick, a reporter from the Cleveland CBS affiliate. She and a cameraman arrived that afternoon. Tall and lovely, Dawn put us at ease with her warm smile.

When Dawn and the cameraman entered Dillie's room, Dillie was standing on her bed. She had heard unfamiliar voices downstairs and was on alert, listening for any indication of danger.

Dawn reached out to pet her. "Well, hello, Dillie. . . ."

Dillie started licking her fingers. It was love at first lick.

Dawn was wearing a flowery perfume that Dillie could not resist. She kept licking Dawn's hands, her face, her hair, and her skirt. When Dawn backed out of the shot so the cameraman could film, Dillie followed her.

"She's so sweet!" Dawn said with delight.

"That's what she's thinking about you," Steve replied.

"She is the most loving creature," I said. "We call her 'Love on Hooves.'"

"Do you think you can get her to jump back up on the bed?" the cameraman asked. "I'd like to film the actual jump."

"Now that she's up," Steve answered, "she'll probably eat her lunch and go outside, then she'll come back up here to sleep."

Dillie followed us down the stairs. She wasn't going to let Dawn, that fragrant flower, get away!

Steve made spaghetti for Dillie to lure her back to her bed, figuring that only her favorite food could make her forget about Dawn's perfume

Back upstairs, Dawn and the cameraman tried to get a shot of Dillie jumping up on the bed.

Dillie refused to follow direction. Steve tried to entice her with some roses, but even her favorite flower was no match for that perfume. Finally, Dawn and her cameraman gave up. They had to get back to Cleveland to edit the footage. Their spot was slated to appear on the six o'clock news—only a few hours away.

As they drove down the driveway, Dillie promptly jumped up on the bed.

"Figures," I said. "What a diva."

Just to prove the point, Dillie jumped off and on the bed again.

"There goes the money shot!" Steve said.

Chapter 26

Fifteen Minutes

Dillie's story went viral the moment it hit the airwaves. People all over the world wanted to hear a story that made them smile. Before Dillie, the most famous animal in the tiny village of Canal Fulton was a chicken with two heads. Now, Dillie was the talk of the town. I headed down to my clinic that morning as if nothing had changed. I had work to do. I was amused that Dillie was now famous, but I had a full appointment schedule of sick pets that meant just as much to their owners as Dillie did to us. To emphasize that point, as soon as I hit the door, my associate Stacy informed me that my hairdresser had just dropped off her large boxer, Diesel. She had told Stacy he was walking very stiffly. Stacy was starting her surgeries for the day and hadn't had time to examine Diesel.

I turned to my assistant, Curtis. "Let's get Diesel done before the appointments start."

When Curtis walked Diesel out from his kennel, I could see why Amy was concerned. As he walked, Diesel kept both back legs rigid. Examining him more closely, I could also see that the individual muscles of both back legs were twitching uncontrollably.

Diesel was a very friendly, large dog. As he got excited to see us, rapidly wagging his tail stub, the muscle twitching worsened. He went completely stiff in both back legs, in a severe muscle spasm. The exam table shook as his muscles twitched. I also noted two distinct puncture marks on the dog's right thigh. All the pieces were beginning to fit into place.

While I sat in the salon chair getting my hair cut, my stylist always talked about her animals. I knew she had a barn with cows, horses, and an undetermined number of barn cats. Diesel frequently visited the barn, trying to catch the cats. Judging from Diesel's parallel puncture wounds, I surmised that one of the cats had caught him.

Cats' teeth are like hypodermic needles, and they inject bacteria from the environment deep into the tissue, where little oxygen can reach. One particular bacteria thrives in barns, requires little oxygen, and produces a potent neuromuscular toxin causing rigid muscle paralysis.

"This dog has tetanus," I told Curtis. I had only seen two other tetanus cases in my career, but Diesel's signs were unmistakable.

"What? I thought dogs didn't get tetanus," he said.

"They do. It's just rare," I went on to explain, "But they

certainly can get it if a cat injects the bacteria right into their thigh."

"That will teach you, Diesel." Curtis scolded the rigid dog. "Leave those cats alone!"

As we loaded Diesel up with the necessary antitoxin, antibiotics, and muscle relaxants, my receptionist Alicin handed me twenty Post-it notes.

"These are all reporters," she said. "Everyone is calling about Dillie."

At my desk over my lunch break, I worked through the stack of Post-it notes.

By the middle of the afternoon, I was exhausted from the Dillie calls, and became a vet again. Diesel was already looking better. That gave me much greater satisfaction than Dilliemania ever could.

"No more calls about Dillie, Alicin," I told our receptionist.

Still, she knocked on the exam room door while I was in the middle of an exam and said, "You have to take this phone call. It's CBS," Alicin replied. "They want you to be on their morning show."

At six o'clock the next morning, a satellite truck and two other vehicles with cameramen and crew rolled up the bumpy driveway to our house. There was a lot of preparation before the actual shoot. This was going to be a live telecast, so Dillie, Steve, and I had to wait. Dillie was being unusually cooperative. As we waited for filming to start, Steve and I sat in the small piano room. Enticed by some vanilla hand lotion, an irresistible treat, Dillie stayed with us.

I noticed that Dillie kept looking anxiously across the

dining room to her potty area and the mats she used like a litter box.

"I think she has to relieve herself," I said. "But if we let her out of the room, we might not be able to get her back."

A production assistant brought Dillie's toilet mat into the room. She immediately lifted her tail and did what she had trained herself to do. One of the crew swept up the droppings.

The interview went by in a flash, and the crew gathered up their equipment. They took selfies with Dillie as they headed out the door.

It was still early, so I headed to the clinic. When I arrived, it seemed as if the whole world had seen the morning show. Enterprising reporters and media agents from all over were calling. Apparently, they had Googled my name and found the clinic's phone number. Fourteen fluorescent orange Post-it notes were stuck to my computer monitor. There were "call me" notes from every local Cleveland station, several animal-themed blogs, and news agencies in England, France, Belgium, and Brazil. I tried to call them all back in between patients, repeating Dillie's story again and again.

"Great," I told Steve when I got home that night. "I am now a famous Internet kook. All the things I have done in my life, all the patients I have saved, and this is my fifteen minutes."

"Just remember," Steve counseled, "that for every story we do, people are out there smiling, all because of our little girl."

One night in January 2010, I took a call before heading up to bed.

"Hi, this is Mark Zinni, from Fox, channel eight," said a youthful, energetic voice.

He wanted to film a segment on Dillie, but with a twist: A webcam would be set up in her room so viewers could watch her after the story.

"Are you kidding?" I asked. "Do you think people really want to watch her sit on her bed and drool?"

"Oh yes!" Mark answered. "People will love it. We're going to make Dillie a star!"

It took a few days for me to piece together a webcam system. I found an international server online that allowed me to broadcast for free. I was shocked when I saw what other people broadcast on their cams.

"Look at this," I said to Steve as I showed him some of the raunchier feeds. "Are we sure we really want the same people who watch cams like this watching Dillie?"

"The people who watch these cams will get bored with her in a second," Steve replied. "Don't worry. After a week or two, we can go back to our normal lives."

With the webcam up and running, Mark and his cameraman came down from Cleveland to film their clip. Mark was an animal lover. He melted when he met Dillie. She stood on the bed and posed for the camera like a pro. Mark fed Dillie roses on camera, which she gobbled up in a single chomp.

The Cleveland Fox station publicized the DillieCam, and Dillie started getting thousands of hits. I received countless e-mails and letters thanking Steve and me for saving Dillie and sharing her story. Many of the letters were in children's scrawls and included crayon pictures of Dillie. One drawing showed Dillie wearing stiletto heels with a note from the child's mother explaining that her child thought Dillie's hooves looked like high heels. Another mother wrote that her autistic child watched Dillie and petted her through the computer screen.

We also got letters from Dillie-watching adults. A woman from Brazil wrote that, because she lived in a city, she never got to see wildlife and really loved tuning in to watch Dillie every day, even though Dillie's life was hardly wild. A fraternity from England wrote that Dillie was now their official mascot. A group of Internet fantasy gamers made Dillie an honorary princess in their league.

Even animals seemed to watch the DillieCam. I received an e-mail from a cat owner whose cat watched Dillie. Attached was a photo of the cat intently staring at the computer screen showing Dillie on her bed.

Steve was the driving force behind the webcam. Seeing the positive response made him want to do more. He staged events on camera, such as feeding Dillie treats with whipped cream that she splashed all over the place. Once a day, with Screamie perched on his shoulder, he groomed Dillie in full view of the entire Web. Dillie licked his hands and kissed his cheeks as she always did. Screamie would waddle slowly down Steve's arm and peck Dillie on the nose.

For Steve, the ultimate prize was making it into *Ripley's Believe It or Not.* "I never told you this," he confessed, "but that has been a lifelong goal of mine, to be in *Ripley's*. Dillie made my dream come true."

People all over the world now knew Dillie. The DillieCam registered more than a thousand hits a day, and hundreds of people friended Dillie on her Facebook page. Many of Dillie's fans became personal friends. Steve and I met artists, photographers, musicians, reporters, and animal lovers from around the globe because of our deer. It didn't matter that all these people came from different professions, social circles, or countries. Love was the universal language, and Dillie was fluent in love.

Chapter 27

Dillie-mania Is Out of This World

Dillie is a creature of habit. Once set in a routine, she adheres to it with military precision. Wake up Daddy: 0500. Bang head on shower door while Daddy gets dressed: 0530. Go outside, walk around yard with Daddy, and eat hay until 0830. Recline in bed until snack and potty time, 1400. Return to bed until evening sentry duty, walking the fence line. Then back in for chow and family bonding time. Back to bed, 1700. Her webcam viewers in the Swiss Army could have tested the accuracy of their precision watches by Dillie's routine. Every now and then, she would change her entire day without warning. For a time, she decided to sleep downstairs by the piano. She slept on the floor next to her bed for several months one year. And, to my dismay, she would occasionally return to our bed.

Whenever Dillie went off-camera for a while, my e-mail lit up with frantic messages, in fourteen different languages, from Dillie viewers all over the world, asking, "Where's Dillie?"

"Is she okay?"

"What's wrong with her?"

One fateful morning, her routine changed radically. Dillie had been lounging in bed, and two women from town had come to visit her. Steve brought them up to her room. Dillie stood and stretched. As she greeted the ladies with kisses and licks, she suddenly jumped off the bed and bolted to the other bedroom, tail up and twitching, then back to her room. She was terrified. Panting and shaking her ears, she bent nearly in half to scratch at her face with a back hoof.

Steve found the lifeless body of a tiny honeybee without its stinger lying on Dillie's bed.

Dillie bolted downstairs and slammed into the back door window. Steve let her outside, where she raced around, terrified, and scratched her head, shaking it from side to side. She stopped occasionally to catch her breath, then began to run all over again. Her panic continued, while Lady and the other animals watched calmly.

After waiting hours for the spooked deer to quiet down, Steve finally called me at work. "We have a problem," he said when I answered the phone.

He explained what had happened and expressed his fear that Dillie was going to injure herself.

I grabbed an auto-injector used for a specific brand of cat vaccine and filled one of the modified syringes with sedative. I could administer only one small dose with the device, but I would be able to pop the drug into Dillie as she ran by. This improvised method seemed like the only way to sedate our terrified deer before she got hurt.

When I arrived home, Dillie was still in panic mode, running up and down the stairs, in and out of each room, jumping on and off the beds. She was overheated and panting, and her fur still stood on end. She didn't stop shaking her head and ears. If she remained still for a moment, she would return to scratching her face with her back hoof.

"Once I sedate her," I told Steve, "we have to lay her down in a contained area. We don't want her falling down the stairs."

We herded Dillie into the piano room, where we had covered the floor with soft mats and blankets. Dillie paced in tight circles. I popped her with the sedative-filled injector pen. The minuscule amount of sedative in the pen would not have slowed most deer her size, but Dillie's reaction was extra-sensitive. The tiny dose knocked her out nicely, and she lay down and went to sleep.

I propped Dillie's head up on a teddy bear to avoid her inhaling any saliva or cud—aspiration could be fatal—and watched the steady rise and fall of her side as she snored softly. I gave her a dose of cortisone to treat her possible allergic reaction to the bee sting, then covered her with a blanket and sat with her, hoof in hand, until she woke up.

As I sat there holding Dillie's hoof, I thought about the thousands of messages Dillie would get from all over the world if she failed to appear on her bed at two p.m. I wondered how I would have handled telling all the people who follow Dillie on the webcam if she had died. I felt over-whelmed. Just then, Steve appeared in the doorway to see how Dillie was doing and found me in tears.

"What's wrong?" he asked. "She's okay, isn't she?"

"She's fine," I answered. "I am a wreck."

Steve sat down next to Dillie and me, and placed one hand on my back and one on Dillie's soft, velvety fur.

The little bee sting altered Dillie's patterns for a long time. Although her daily routine continued with the same military precision, Dillie avoided her bed for months. Instead of using the bed, she retreated to the closet in the master bedroom.

Dillie obviously connected her bedroom with the bee sting. She also associated any lotion or flowery perfume, which her visitors must have been wearing, with the episode. Any contact with the fragrant product she used to love triggered a panic reaction. She fluffed up her fur, shook her ears, scratched her face, and raced back and forth. We started warning visitors not to wear perfume or scented lotions.

When my cousin Jennifer came to visit, Dillie's panic reaction kicked in. Dillie kept nosing Jennifer's purse. When Jennifer searched inside, she located the offending object: a tube of lip balm, made of natural beeswax. The problem was the beeswax, not a flowery fragrance.

Not only did we have restrictions for visitors but also while Dillie slept in our room again, Steve and I let the camera go dark. Immediately, we were deluged with frantic e-mails and messages.

One e-mail shocked me. It read, "Whaaaaa. Where's Dillie?" and was signed "the International Space Station."

"Are you kidding me?" Steve said when I told him Dillie had a message from outer space. He was outside with Dillie, playing their bullfighting game. He rubbed her ears as she licked his hands. "You are an intergalactic star now, Dillie!"

Steve persuaded me to set up the webcam in Dillie's new bivouac in our closet. When her fans could view their favorite deer once again, the frantic messages stopped.

On one particularly hot evening, I got up from bed to open a window. Dillie was lying down in the closet, contentedly chewing her cud. Startled by the sound of the window being opened, she jumped up, bolted into her room, and leaped onto her bed, as if nothing had ever happened.

Chapter 28

Love on Hooves

From the night I sat on the floor holding Dillie's hoof, I had not been able to shake the desire to return to our quiet life. I was ready to pull the DillieCam's plug.

Five years after we started Elm Ridge, Dean retired again, prompted by the sudden death of a good friend. He said it was a wakeup call for him to spend more time with his family. I was beginning to understand Dean's desire to change the pace of his life.

As I went to my computer to shut down the webcam, Steve appeared, holding some mail.

"Look at this card she got today," he said, handing me the card.

The envelope had been addressed to:

Dillie the Deer,
Canal Fulton, Ohio 44614

The two-person staff at the local post office knew where Dillie lived. The postwoman delivered it to the front door and came inside to visit the star.

The card read:

Dear Dillie and Family,

    Thank you for bringing a smile to my mother's face. She is fighting cervical cancer, and watching you helps her deal with chemotherapy.

    Thank you, Dillie. You give her so much peace.

"You see," Steve said, "it's our duty to do this, our mission. This is how we share God's love, how we teach others about love."

Card in hand, I sat on the bed next to Dillie. Lady looked up lazily, then went back to sleep. Spazz stretched his paws up to the ceiling. Neffie nuzzled Dillie, cradled under her long, folded legs. Dillie licked my face.

Steve took a seat on the side of the bed. When she looked at him, Dillie's eyes lit up like a summer sky. She laid her head in his lap, wiggled her ears, and licked his hand.

I thought about how much our lives were enriched because of this beautiful animal. I recalled the anxious first days, not knowing if Dillie was going to live. Her first swim in the pool. The day she discovered spaghetti. The toothpaste wars. Finding her splashing in the bubble bath.

In that instant, I understood why people had become so enchanted by this little deer who should have never survived. Dillie was so beautiful, so peaceful, and so serene. She was the embodiment of joy. Her survival had been a miracle of love, and every molecule in her body displayed the glory of creation. This beautiful animal returned the love that saved her every day, delivering it to all the corners of the globe on her dainty cloven hooves.

I had to agree with Steve. Our mission was to spread the love of the Creator and the beauty of the animal spirit. We had been given this honor and had an obligation to continue, no matter how much trouble it caused us.

Chapter 29

Survivor's Spirit

As summer was winding down in August 2010, the pace of our lives grew even more hectic. Dillie-mania had mushroomed. The number of webcam viewers broke a million. Dillie appeared on shows in South Korea, France, Belgium, and Germany, and stacks of mail deluged the office from around the world.

"Dillie needs a personal assistant," Steve muttered as he sorted through more than two dozen cards the postman had just delivered. He turned to Curtis, one of the assistants at the clinic, and said, "Do I have a job for you!"

We were all aware that nothing could be less appealing to Curtis. The former college football player, who could bench press a Yugo, had a secret fear. Deer terrified him.

Being offered a job as Dillie's personal assistant, even as a joke, was not a welcome prospect. "No, thanks," he told Steve. "I would rather be Willie Nelson's barber."

"Come on, Curtis," I said. "You could be her personal hoof waxer."

"No way!" he said with a shudder. "She'd kill me."

I found it hard to believe that Curtis was afraid of a gentle animal like Dillie. He routinely wrestled some of the meanest dogs in our practice without a shred of fear. In fact, the first case of the morning was a 130-pound German shepherd named Max, who tried to kill us all. Curtis hung on to him without losing patience or his grip.

"Not a very good way to start the day," I remarked after the exam. It was going to be a challenging morning. We worked at full throttle, and then our lunch break was interrupted by an emergency heatstroke case. By the end of the day, we were ragged. I was relieved when it was time to lock up.

As I was saying good-bye to Curtis and Sally, our receptionist, a car pulled up with a loud squeal. One of our clients ran to the clinic entrance, holding the family's tiny, red miniature dachshund, Ginger, wrapped in a blanket. Only her head and wagging tail were visible. After she parked their car, which was packed for vacation, his wife raced to join us.

Curtis reached for Ginger, who snarled and snapped.

"She's ripped open," her frantic owner said. "She was attacked by another dog."

His wife pulled back the blood-soaked blanket.

Curtis and I gasped.

The little dog, still alert, was torn open from the base of her pelvis all the way to her diaphragm. Her spleen, bladder, and entire small intestine were loose in the blanket. She also had large lacerations on both sides of her chest, from which a small piece of pink lung popped out when she inhaled.

"Can you save her?" her owner pleaded.

I wondered how Ginger could possibly survive such severe injuries, but I knew not to underestimate an animal's ability to overcome even the worst possible circumstances and resolved to save the spunky dog.

"All we can do is try," I said. "We have to take Ginger to surgery immediately. Do you want us to attempt to save her?"

"Yes," both owners said simultaneously.

Even though it was closing time and this was a case for the emergency clinic, Ginger's condition was too critical to send her to the ER, which was five miles away.

"Can you stay, Curtis?" I asked. "She has to go right to surgery."

"Absolutely," he responded without hesitation. Curtis moved Ginger back to surgery and started prepping her for an IV catheter.

I told the owners we would be tied up in surgery for a few hours and promised to call them as soon as I could. I left them with Sally to sign consent forms and then joined Curtis in the surgery room.

Ginger's blood loss and dire injuries were overwhelming her. She lay limply on the surgery table as Curtis and I placed the IV and administered her anesthetics.

"We can't clip or scrub her, Curtis," I told him. "Her

abdomen's wide open. We can only use saline on her. We're just going to blast her with antibiotics and pray to the Holy Mother of Peritonitis that we can get this under control. Infection is the least of her worries right now."

The tears in Ginger's chest prevented her from breathing normally on her own.

Once Ginger was sedated and intubated, Curtis breathed for her by squeezing the balloon-like rebreathing bag on the anesthetic machine to force air in and out of her lungs. Sally came back to fill us in on the details of Ginger's traumatic night. The owners were planning to leave Ginger with a friend who had a golden retriever while they were on vacation. They'd dropped Ginger off, left the dogs in the fenced-in backyard, and had gone around to the driveway to say good-bye. When the friends returned to the yard, they found their retriever mauling Ginger. Ginger's owners, excited to be off on their trip, hadn't made it down the street before they were called back to the dreadful scene.

Sally asked if I needed her to stay. A great receptionist, unparalleled in befriending and assisting our clients, she couldn't stomach the medical part of our job. Anything we did with the animals made her very squeamish. Since she was not going to be of any help during the surgery, I thanked her for staying and told her to go home.

I began to sort through the bowel. The situation was even worse than I had thought. Grass, sand, and bowel contents coated the organs in and out of Ginger's abdomen.

Just then, we heard the back door swing open. My tech Sherry walked into the operating room. "Heard you might need some help," she said.

Curtis had managed to text her what was happening. She didn't even reply, just jumped in her car and drove to the clinic. I was relieved to have an extra set of hands.

"What do you need me to do?" she asked.

"Well, first of all, please call Steve and tell him I won't be home till late. Then, jump in over here. We need to piece this bowel back together."

Sherry looked over our patient. "Oh my God," she said. "How did this happen?"

"HBGR," Curtis said, using a twist on the acronym HBC (hit by car). "Hit by golden retriever."

The three of us began our surgical repair of Ginger. Since Curtis and I were already scrubbed-in and were wearing masks, gloves, and gowns, Sherry monitored the anesthesia and gathered the necessary sutures, sterile supplies, and medications.

I found two torn blood vessels in the mesentery, the membrane that attaches the intestines to the posterior wall of the abdomen. The blood vessels were actively pumping away, flooding Ginger's abdominal cavity. I quickly threw surgical clamps on them. Running through the damaged bowel, I identified three specific areas that would need to be resected. Intestinal tissue is too delicate for surgical clamps, so Curtis gently held the pieces of damaged intestine in his fingers as I sutured.

"Look at this." He held up a loop of bowel we were going to resect. "That dog actually chewed on Ginger's bowel."

A golden-retriever-size bite mark was in the center of the loop.

"Poor little dog!" She had been mangled by a dog ten times her size, ripped open, and then had watched, helpless, as the golden retriever had chewed on her intestines. Yet she still came into the clinic wagging her tail and showing attitude with a capital A. The injuries were so extreme, I worried that not even Ginger could survive them.

For three hours, we resected and delicately reattached her injured bowel. Curtis and I then meticulously tweezed out every piece of grass, dirt, and hair we could find in the abdominal cavity. We doused the abdomen with warm, sterile saline and antibiotics and pieced the abdominal wall back together, leaving in drains we could use to continue treating the contaminated belly.

I decided not to repair the chest that night. We would do it as a second surgery the following day. The single most dangerous time for Ginger was going to be right after that surgery. As she was, she could expand her lungs, because the free air around the lungs was moving out of her chest cavity through the bite wounds as she breathed. This is known as an open pneumothorax. Once we repaired the holes and made the chest airtight again, the lungs would have a harder time expanding against that free air. She would have a tension pneumothorax, a much more dangerous situation than the open variety. To offset the tension pneumothorax, Curtis and I would place a chest tube and a valve that allowed the air to escape once we closed her chest, pulling that air off her chest and allowing her lungs to expand.

Rather than putting her through more hours of surgery right then, we packed her chest wounds with sterile bandaging that was not airtight and woke her up.

Within minutes of finishing her surgery, Ginger was awake and snarling. I was applying her narcotic patch when she snapped at me. If Sherry had not been restraining Ginger's head, she would have bitten me.

"This dog is one tough cookie," I said with admiration.

The three of us agreed to do the second surgery, on the chest wounds, after business hours the next day, a Saturday.

I called the owners to update them on the condition of their tiny dynamo. Things had gone well so far, but I couldn't help thinking that the worst might be yet to come. We were going to have a battle ahead fighting infection and hoping that the pieced-together bowel held. Ginger was not going to be out of the woods for days.

We packed her up in a laundry basket with her fluids and IV pump, the warmer we had used for baby Dillie six years earlier, and blankets. I decided to take the dachshund home with me that first night. I called Steve to let him know I was bringing home a critical patient. Curtis helped me load her into the car.

Steve was waiting in the driveway when we arrived. He carried Ginger, tucked in the laundry basket, into the house and right up the steps to the bathroom in our bedroom. Dillie was snoozing on her bed and did not notice the little dog passing by. Lady circled the laundry basket, peeking at Ginger.

Ginger responded by snarling.

Once her IV pump was flowing and Ginger was bedded down for the night in our deep whirlpool tub, I finally caught my breath and got ready for bed.

"Tomorrow," I told Steve, as I got under the covers, "we have to take her back to surgery and do her chest wounds."

I got up every two hours to check on the patient, adjust her fluids, and give her her scheduled treatments. Setting an alarm was not necessary. Dillie liked to play in our bathroom every night, opening drawers and jumping in the tub. With her access blocked by the closed door, she head-butted the bathroom door in frustration every few hours. Ginger remained quiet, and Dillie never suspected that an injured dog was now sleeping in her favorite nighttime play palace. When Dillie saw me caring for the little visitor the next morning, she responded with a predictable tail fluff and hoof stomp.

Ginger had done very well through the night, but she appeared to be nauseated. Even a little sip of water caused her to turn her head away and urp. Steve helped me put the laundry basket in the backseat of my car as Lady sniffed it, tail wagging. I took off for the clinic, where the staff could monitor Ginger.

After our scheduled Saturday-morning appointments, Sherry, Curtis, and I began Ginger's chest surgery. I repaired the muscle tears between her ribs, placed a chest tube, and sutured the long, jagged lacerations on both sides of her chest. It was nearly three o'clock when we finished.

I called Ginger's owners and gave them an update. She had gone through surgery two in fine form.

"She's a remarkable dog," I told them.

I consulted with Dean about our patient. "She's still very nauseated," I told him. "Other than that, she is kicking butt and taking names."

Dean asked what type of pain medication I was using.

"A fentanyl patch." Fentanyl is an extremely strong narcotic, which Ginger needed to keep her pain in check.

"That's why she's nauseated," he said. "Once her patch comes off, her nausea will stop."

As always, Dean was spot-on. We removed Ginger's patch the next day, and within a few hours she was eating greedily and never looked back. She was home in her momma's lap a day after that.

Ginger is still a patient. I see her once a year for her annual checkup. She snarls and snaps at me still, but that just makes me smile. She has jagged scars on both sides of her chest, and there is a scar on her long dachshund belly, but these only add to her mystique as far as I'm concerned. Her scars signal that she is a spirited survivor who does not cave in or give up.

Chapter 30

From the Peaks to the Troughs

Dillie's webcam launch and the enthusiastic response from her fans all over the world started 2010 on a high note. But life is a roller coaster. My grandmother Rose, who had been ill, and Pat, my close friend and receptionist, died in 2010. Pat, who had cradled Dillie that first night at the emergency clinic, had developed small cell lung cancer. She had waited too long to see a doctor and passed away soon after her diagnosis.

To add to the sadness of the year, we also lost two of our animal family, Neffie and Screamie. Neffie, our majestic Abyssinian cat, had always been an extraordinary athlete. To keep Lady out of her food, I fed her on top of the refrigerator. She effortlessly jumped from the floor to the top of the fridge every single day. About mid-June of 2010, I realized that she no longer was making that jump. Instead, she jumped to the lower counter and then to the top of the fridge on a second jump.

At first, I just assumed this was a natural result of aging. She was thirteen, no longer a kitten. By the end of summer, I noticed that she was dragging her left foreleg when she walked and was having episodes of disorientation and circling. A slowly progressive brain problem in a cat her age was likely a tumor.

I scheduled an MRI for her at a local veterinary specialty hospital. When her condition deteriorated rapidly, I cancelled the appointment. I couldn't put her through procedures that would be difficult for her just so I could know where the tumor was located. My desire to know the details of her illness was superseded by my respect for her right not to suffer.

When she could not make the jump to the counter, I started to feed her on a low table in the kitchen, just a few feet off the ground. On the last day of her life, she sat on the floor below the table and cried a mournful meow. She could not get on the table. She circled uncontrollably for minutes on end, howling the whole time, then lay down on the floor and seizured.

I knew it was time to end her suffering. With a broken heart, I took her to my office that morning and had Stacy sedate and euthanize our little royal cat.

Just a few months later, Screamie, our colorful, tiny screaming eagle, passed away. When Steve came down the steps that morning, his little yellow companion did not fly to greet him as she always did. He looked in her cage and saw her huddled on the bottom.

He called up the steps to me. "Mel, come down here. Something's wrong with Screamie."

I ran down the steps in my bathrobe to find him holding her in his outstretched hands. She was struggling to breathe. I could see a swelling in her lower belly. She was egg-bound. Egg-binding is a very dangerous situation for a little bird. When a small, single, female bird is strongly attached to her owner, the risk for developing this condition is higher. Screamie had chosen Steve as her mate. When Steve read the newspaper each morning, she would march up and down his arm with her feathers fluffed and wings spread, guarding her beloved. If I got too close to him in her presence, she would fly at me and bite me, much as she treated the other animals in the family.

I watched helplessly as she gasped a few times and died in Steve's hand. He was devastated and sobbed unashamedly.

Dillie, Lady, and Spazz did not seem to notice the absence of Neffie and Screamie. They went about their daily routines as if nothing had changed. Steve and I were grieving all of our losses.

As the animals and people I cherished were taken away, I came to understand that loss was a part of life and just how short life could be. Still, every final good-bye took a piece of my heart. Then, one more sadness shattered me.

On January 26, 2011, my beloved friend and former practice associate Dean fell off a ladder in his home, crushing the vertebrae in his neck. Just like that, he was gone.

Steve and I stood with hundreds of mourners at Dean's funeral in a four-hour line during freezing rain. Many of our clients and colleagues came to me in the line to express their sorrow. Our clients hugged me and shared a story about how Dean had saved their pets when no one else could, or how he had helped them out when no other vet in town would see them.

So many mournful people thanked Dean for the lives he had saved, and placed photos of the pets he used to care for inside the casket.

"Take care of my Scooby for me, Doc," I heard one client say, lovingly placing a photo of a Jack Russell terrier among the hundreds of other pictures.

After Dean's death, I concentrated on my work. I needed to be as good as Dean had been, as gifted and kind. Everything else was just a distraction.

I was feeling more fatigued than usual by the end of 2011. I had a dull but persistent pain in my lower right abdomen, which a daily painkiller muted. As soon as the meds wore off, the pain returned. In my heart, I knew it was cancer. I didn't know what else could cause an abdominal pain that never goes away. I knew not to ignore my suspicions.

My doctor had been a family friend for two decades. Dr. Bob had delivered my niece and nephews.

"Just spay me," I told him. "I think it's cancer."

He laughed. He had a deep laugh and a rich bass voice. He listened to my concerns and never dismissed my fears as hysteria.

On a follow-up visit we discussed the lab reports, and I discovered that he was no better at giving bad news than most doctors. He came into the exam room and said, "Well, kid, you have cancer." He handed me a copy of my lab report.

Seeing my tears, he tried to console me. "Don't worry,"

he said. "It's slow growing. Stage one. No big deal. We'll go in there next week and get it. It'll be like it never happened."

I was reading the report as he spoke. I had to read cytology reports every day for my own patients. Reading about my own condition was different. The test results indicated that I had a hot, malignant cancer. Despite what Dr. Bob had just told me, the pathologist had written that this was an aggressive endometrial carcinosarcoma, which meant that my prognosis was not good.

I looked up at Dr. Bob through my tears. He knew I understood the full scope of the report. "Do I need to see an oncologist?" I asked.

His demeanor changed. The smile was gone. He held my hand. "Yes, I think you should," he said.

I went straight from Dr. Bob's office to Heggy's. Paris has the Louvre, Pisa, the tower, and my home town has Heggy's, a hand-crafted chocolate company with an old style soda fountain. I treated myself to a hot fudge sundae, an indulgence I rarely allowed myself.

I definitely deserved some comfort food. I decided to call Steve from there, because it would be easier to play down the news in a phone conversation. I felt shaky and knew I couldn't handle it when Steve fell apart. I wanted the time leading up to the surgery to be as normal as possible.

I told Steve that I had cancer—that we had caught it early and that surgery would take care of it. I did my best to keep him from overreacting and assured him that everything would be fine. After the initial shock, I think he chose to believe me, because he could not conceive of the alternative. Then I went back to work. I had to get my mind off what I had read in the report.

I stayed awake all that night, trying to figure out what to do. I had no idea how I was going to deal with the disease. I thought I might have to sell the business.

As my mind jumped from one concern to another, I found myself thinking about a dramatic case involving a heroic dog named Sweetheart who came into the clinic on a warm summer night years ago. I had just finished suturing a dog who had gone through a window trying to attack a deliveryman when Sherry burst into the exam room.

"We need you," she said.

I told the dog's owner to keep him from chewing his stitches and excused myself.

My next patient was propped upright on her side in the treatment area. She was a medium-size Australian shepherd mixed breed with thick fur. Her head was down, and she did not look up when I walked in. All black except for a white heart-shaped spot on her forehead, she was covered in blood. Her bulging abdomen revealed she was pregnant, with a large litter due any day.

My crew was already clipping her for an IV.

"She's very cold," Sherry said. "Definitely in shock."

"What happened to her?" I asked, putting on my stethoscope. "Hit by a car?"

Sherry turned the gurney around so I could see the dog's other side. The six-inch wooden handle of a large kitchen knife protruded from her ample belly.

"Oh dear God!" I said.

The dog had stab wounds all over her chest and belly.

She had lacerations on her face, and her right lip was shredded and bleeding heavily. She was breathing in heavy, painful gasps. I knew she was bleeding internally by the color of her gums. Her labored breaths revealed that her lungs had been punctured, and air was leaking into her chest, producing a life-threatening condition, pneumothorax,

I grabbed a butterfly set and started pulling air out of the dog's chest as fast as I could. The leaking air was filling her chest cavity, crushing her lungs. We needed to get the excess air out of there or she would die in minutes.

"Get some oxygen for her," I told the staff. "Put a second IV in her jugular. Biggest cath you can fit in. Fluids full blast. Saline on a blood set. Get a double unit of packed cell blood warmed up ASAP."

I had already pulled two liters of air from her chest, but the shepherd was still struggling to breathe. The chest tap and oxygen mask kept her from immediate respiratory arrest, but she was still in grave danger.

I had to consult with the dog's owner, Mr. Ross, about what he wanted to do. She needed emergency surgery, but would probably die regardless. She was bleeding out fast.

"Clip up her belly," I told Sherry. "If the owner okays it, we are going in now. Leave the knife in place till we have her on the table."

Mr. Ross was slumped over in a chair in the first exam cottage. He was skinny, about my age, and wore jeans and a blood-spattered Cleveland Indians T-shirt. His hands were bandaged with blood-soaked tube socks.

I introduced myself quickly. "You need to go to the hospital," I said, after a closer look at his wounded hands.

"It's just a couple of cuts," he muttered, dismissing my concern. "I had to get her here first. She's much worse than I am."

This devoted man, who was shaking in his seat, touched me. I was prepared to go all out to save his dog.

"Her condition is critical," I explained. "We have to get to work on her immediately. I am sorry, but I don't know her name."

"Her name is Sweetheart," he said. "She's got a heart-shaped mark on her head. That's how she got her name."

"I saw that. What happened to her?"

"It was my son," he said in a quaking voice. "He came after me. He started stabbing me. Sweetheart saved me." Tears fell down his blood-spattered face. "He would have killed me," Mr. Ross continued. "She's ready to pop with puppies, and she attacked him, biting his legs. He turned on her and started stabbing, and stabbing, and . . ."

My receptionist Pat came into the room with the chart and a box of Kleenex.

"Even after all he did to Sweetheart, she kept on attacking him. She chased him right out of the house with that knife sticking out of her. You've got to save her, Doc."

"We'll try," I said. "We're taking her to surgery right now."

"I know she's bad, Doc," Mr. Ross said. "But I owe her the chance. If you can't save her, please try to save her puppies."

"We will." I headed to the treatment area with Pat.

"What about an estimate?" she asked. "Do you need a deposit?"

I shook my head. "Just have him sign permission for surgery, okay? And get him to go to the hospital."

Mr. Ross's story was disturbing, but I had to focus on Sweetheart and her unborn puppies.

The staff had Sweetheart on the surgery prep table, IV flowing, blood on board, belly clipped. We moved the unconscious dog to the surgery table and laid her on her back. She was fading fast. I injected the local anesthetic, and Sherry started to do a surgical scrub on the incision site.

"There's no time," I said. "I'm just going to go right in. He wants us to save the pups."

We couldn't transfuse blood fast enough to make up for what Sweetheart had lost. She still had a heartbeat, but that was all. I pulled out the knife embedded in her stomach. The blade was ten inches long.

I cut open Sweetheart's abdomen while the staff tied her down on the table and hooked up the monitors. Her uterus had been sliced open, and puppies in their birth sacs floated freely in her blood. There were more puppies than I could count.

"Get everyone in here," I told Sherry. "There's a truckload of puppies!" To save them, we were going to need every person at the clinic.

During most C-sections, I break open a puppy's birth sac, clamp off the umbilical cord, and drop the puppy into an assistant's hands. The tech then invigorates the puppy by rubbing her, suctioning her mouth and nose, tying off her cord, and making sure she can breathe on her own.

This was not a normal C-section. Some of the puppies had been stabbed, and one of them decapitated. I started pulling out puppies as fast as I could. Every staff member was working on at least two puppies simultaneously. Even

Sherry, who was pumping the rebreathe bag on the anesthesia machine to keep Sweetheart breathing, was reviving two puppies between breaths.

C-section puppies are normally somewhat sedated, but Sweetheart had not had general anesthesia. As a result, her puppies were lively. Many of them squirmed in their sacs. I soon heard the cries of newborn puppies as my staff cared for them.

"Her heart just stopped," Sherry said as I pulled out the last puppy.

Sweetheart's belly was wide open, and I could see the knife wounds in her shredded diaphragm. I reached into her chest and began cardiac massage. We administered medications directly into her heart, but she did not come back. She had survived long enough for all of her puppies to be born. Those puppies would never know their mother.

"What a dog," I said.

Puppies squealed everywhere.

"How many are there?" I asked.

"We've got fifteen," Pat said. "Five are dead."

I looked at the ten living puppies. Many of them had superficial knife wounds that required a few quick surgical staples. They were all breathing well except for one little girl who was gasping for life in Rhonda's hands.

"We have to save that one," I told Rhonda. "Look at her head."

All the puppies were jet black, but this one had a white heart on her forehead, just like her mom. I gave the puppy puffs of oxygen and injected epinephrine and a respiratory stimulant through her umbilical vein.

Rhonda placed the pup under the electric hand dryer by the scrub sink. "Look, Doc," she said over the loud whoosh of the dryer. "She's breathing better."

I knew it was likely that Mr. Ross would want to see Sweetheart, so I sutured her belly. The staff moved her body to a gurney and placed the dead puppies beside her. We covered her with a blanket and waited for Mr. Ross to return from the hospital.

A policeman appeared before he did. We showed the officer the knife, and he shook his head. He told us that this wasn't the first time he had responded to calls from the Ross home. Mr. Ross's son, who was only seventeen, was a violent schizophrenic. He was under a doctor's care but did not always take his medicine. The officer said the family never pressed charges.

"I hope they do this time," he said. "That kid needs serious help or he is going to kill someone."

Pat took me aside.

"There's a client named Judy Deeds in room two who's been here an hour," she said. "She thinks the garage door fell on her cat. Her cat looks stable, but no one's been able to check her in."

As the officer took photos and wrote out his report, I moved on with my night.

Judy Deeds, a middle-aged woman in a wheelchair, was accompanied by her teenage daughter, who was texting two-handed and ignoring everything else. She didn't even look up as I entered.

"Sorry about the wait," I said as I introduced myself. "We had fifteen puppies to deliver."

"Your receptionist told me what happened. Did everyone make it?" Judy asked, concerned.

"Unfortunately, no. Mom and five of the puppies did not survive."

"Oh, that's so sad," she said.

"So, your cat was caught in the garage door?"

"Well, we think that's what happened," Judy said. "She's been crawling around crying all day and walking funny."

Her daughter looked up from her phone and joined the conversation as she took the young calico cat out of her carrier. "Yeah, she just keeps sticking her butt up in the air, see?" She placed the cat on the floor, and the cat did just as she described, purring and cooing all the while.

I smiled. This was an easy one. I looked at the chart in earnest for the first time. Princess the cat, who was now rolling all over the floor, was six months old.

I picked up Princess and placed her on the exam table. I did an obligatory exam, but I knew the diagnosis. "Have you ever had a cat before?" I asked.

"No," Judy said. "I do a lot of dog rescue, but this is our first cat."

"Well, this is good news. She's in heat. This is how cats act when they're in heat."

Both mother and daughter were shocked. "Oh my God," Judy said. "I am so sorry to waste your time."

"Don't be," I answered. "This is much better than spinal trauma."

The clinic got cases like this about five times a year. I never charged for a "heat emergency." We used the time to encourage the owners to have the cat spayed as soon as possible.

"Doctor," Judy asked, "could we see some of the puppies? I used to do dog rescue all the time, till my MS got worse. I miss puppies."

"Sure," I said. I had Rhonda bring in the basket of ten puppies, all snoozing soundly.

Judy stroked each puppy. Her daughter even put away her phone to cuddle some of them.

Princess the cat was also interested in the puppies. She peered into the basket, slowly reached out a paw, and touched one. She started to crawl into the basket with them, but Judy stopped her.

"Someone's ready to be a mom," I said.

"Hand-raising this many puppies is a lot of work," Judy said. "If the owner needs any help with them, I'd be happy to volunteer."

Just as she finished making her offer, I saw Mr. Ross walk into the lobby with freshly bandaged hands.

"He's here right now," I said. "I'll talk to him about it and let you know what he says."

Pat showed Mr. Ross into the client lounge, a quiet, comfortable area we used to give owners a private place to grieve.

I met him in there and told him that Sweetheart had died. I broke the news as gently as I could, emphasizing that she passed peacefully after the last puppy was delivered.

"She was a true hero, Mr. Ross," I said.

"Can I see her?" he asked.

We brought in Sweetheart's body, wrapped in a clean blanket, and let him have time alone with her. "Just tap on the door when you're ready," I said.

I could hear his sobs through the closed door.

When he tapped, we wheeled out his beloved Sweetheart.

"She had ten puppies that lived," I said. "Do you want to see them?"

"What am I going to do with them?" he asked. "I can't have them around my son. I can't take care of them. Do you know a rescue that will take them?"

"Well . . . ," I said slowly. Judy and her daughter were chatting with Pat at the front desk. Sometimes God drops a solution out of the sky.

Judy and Mr. Ross bonded immediately, and exchanged names and contact information. Judy agreed to pick up the puppies in the morning and take them home. She promised to raise the puppies and to keep one herself, to train as a service dog.

After Judy left, we moved Sweetheart to Mr. Ross's car. "Doc," he said apologetically, "I left without a checkbook. Can you just send me a bill?"

"Pay what you can, when you can," I told him. "Thank you for the honor of meeting Sweetheart."

A few months later, I received a very sad handwritten letter. Mr. Ross thanked me for trying so hard to save Sweetheart, but said that his son's legal and medical bills had ruined him, and he could not pay his bill. He wrote:

> If there is any good that came out of this, it is that Judy and I have become friends. I got to see the puppies grow up.

Judy had kept her promise. She and her daughter had

a wonderful time raising the puppies together. Nine of the puppies were placed in other loving homes. As promised, she kept the last puppy to train as a service dog. Mr. Ross described the dog in his note:

> That one is her pride and joy. Smart as a whip.
> > It's the pup with the white heart on her forehead.
> > She's named Sweetheart, too.

As I lay in bed dreading the coming days, I was inspired by Sweetheart's bravery, Mr. Ross's perseverance, and Judy's kindness. They salvaged goodness and grace from Sweetheart's grisly death. Though it might prove difficult, I had to try to find goodness and grace in my battle with cancer.

Dillie jumped on the bed at that moment, as she used to when she was younger. She plunked down between me and Steve and laid her head on my shoulder. She always seemed to know when I was struggling. I put my arm around her and let her stay.

My cell phone lit up with messages from concerned webcam viewers. "Where's Dillie?" they asked. We had grown to understand that some of the people fixated on Dillie's webcam were dependent on her. When she was not available, they panicked. One of them texted me once when our power was out in a storm.

"Where's Dillie??"

"Tornado warning," I texted back. "Power out. We are in the basement."

Her response: "Please let me know when she is back on."

Tonight, Dillie was with me, and I wasn't letting go.

Chapter 31

It's All About the Chemo

When I had my first surgery in 2012, I was laid up for about a month. Lady would not leave my side. If I was resting, she was in bed next to me. If I had to use the bathroom, she followed me in there. Dillie lay next to the bed or the recliner I sat in. If I wasn't feeling well, Lady and Dillie were always within an arm's reach, to offer comfort by staying near and not demanding anything. On the other hand, Spazz, being a cat, mostly kept his distance. With my animal support group, I recuperated well and was glad to get back to work

I was due for some good news. After thirty-eight consecutive days of radiation therapy, my first scans showed that I was tumor-free. The hardest part of the radiation treatment was lying still for thirty minutes each day. Though

I was crazy busy, I started each day strapped to a table, lying perfectly still. I had a million things to do. I continued to work hard at Elm Ridge with the help of Dr. Stacy Bridges. Stacy and her husband, Mike, worked for me before they were vets. I had a full roster of patients who needed care, blood work to review, clients to talk to, employees to manage, and bills to pay. I had all the hubbub going on with Dillie. I had lectures to prepare for a night class I was teaching. I was designing a lost-and-found database for pets in the area and revamping the database for the emergency clinic.

I scheduled the radiation therapy as early in the day as I could and left Steve at home to carry on the morning routine with Dillie, Lady, and Spazz. I didn't want to disrupt their schedule and the rhythm of their lives. I also began to enjoy the quiet time alone before what inevitably evolved into a demanding day.

During my radiation treatments, I passed the time by imagining I was having a conversation with my dearly departed friends Pat and Dean. I missed them both terribly, and it was therapeutic for me to think of them and pretend Pat was telling me a joke or Dean was counseling me about a case. At first, I had to force myself to think about them, but by the end of the month, as soon as I got strapped onto the table, they were right there, eager to talk to me, and they made the time fly by. People I loved had been taken away so quickly. Imagining my old friends keeping me company helped me cope with my boredom, frustration, and uncertainty.

In October, about a month after completing the radiation protocol, I felt a familiar pain in my gut. I knew the tumor was back. The radiation doctor tried to convince me it was the gallstones they had seen on the scans, and sent me to a surgeon to have my gallbladder removed. When I met with the surgeon, I asked him to take a look around when he was in there with the endoscope. The surgeon laughed at my fears.

I was absolutely convinced that I would die, that all the treatment I was undergoing was just postponing the inevitable. But I wasn't afraid of dying. After all, every one of us is going to die. I just wanted my life to matter in the vast scheme of the universe.

After the surgery, I woke up in the recovery room to find the surgeon standing over me.

"You're right. It's cancer," I heard him say through the fog of sedation. "We didn't remove your gallbladder." They had gone in with the scope and found a five-centimeter mass to the right of the entry point, right where my pain was.

"While we were in there," he continued, "we pulled up your CT scans from just a month ago, and this wasn't there. This is a hot one."

The surgeon said he was going out to the waiting area to tell my family.

I stopped him. "No," I said. "I will."

I wiped away my tears. *Brave face forward,* I thought.

My heart broke when Steve bounced out of his chair with a big smile on his face.

"That was quick!" he said.

My dad and his wife, Reva, joined him.

"That wasn't so bad, was it?" my father asked in his booming voice.

My resolve vanished, and I started to cry. "The cancer's back," I blurted out.

Steve was in denial on the way home. "They're not really sure it's cancer," he said. "They didn't biopsy it. Maybe it's just scar tissue."

I called the radiation doctor from the car, leaving a voice mail message with the day's bad news. In less than two minutes, he called me back. I told him the surgeon had ordered CT scans the next week.

A week later, the radiation doctor called with the results. "There are three masses," he told me. "It's all about the chemo now."

When I met with the surgeon some weeks later, he told me that the latest scans brought worse news: The cancer had spread. There were tumors in my kidneys, liver, lungs, and even bones.

This news knocked the air right out of me. I could barely speak. I assured him that my specialist had made the necessary arrangements for chemotherapy.

"Good," the surgeon said. "Go home and get your affairs in order."

In my brief experience as a cancer patient, my doctors had handled giving me bad news terribly. They initially sugar-coated what they had to say. Of course, I wouldn't let them, I was a medical professional after all. If they glossed over any of the facts or put what seemed to be too positive a spin on my condition, I pressed them for the hard truth. I wanted to know what I was dealing with. But, when the surgeon told me to get my affairs in order, I felt as if I had been hit over the head with a hammer. I was horrified by the thought of masses growing everywhere in my body.

I did not tell Steve how widely the cancer had spread. Just knowing the cancer had returned had destroyed him.

"What am I going to do without you?" he asked through his tears, sobbing like a child.

His fear made me stronger, because I had to pretend there was nothing to be afraid of. I protected him from dealing with the medical establishment. He drove me to my appointments, but, at my request, rarely stayed. Steve is the most impatient person on the planet. I didn't want to be with him if there might be a wait. He was too emotional to be with me for the consultations. I didn't want him to hear about my condition unfiltered.

"I'm going to be just fine. Nothing's changed. It's all about the chemo now," I said, repeating my doctor's words, even though I didn't believe them. And I knew the doctor didn't either.

I couldn't sleep. I had a lot to do.

The surgeon had told me to get my affairs in order. When we got home, I went to my upstairs office to do just that. Lady painfully made her way up the stairs behind me. She had always been so energetic, but she was suddenly showing her age. She was moving much more slowly. Lady was finding it hard to jump up on the couch to watch TV, and we had started having to help her up on the bed at night.

Lady sat by my desk as I thought about the coming chemotherapy and what I had to do to prepare for the future. I patted my lap and she rested her head on my thighs with some difficulty.

"Lady, old girl," I said to her, "we're both falling apart, but we will get through this together, I promise."

Lady curled up at my feet.

I knew that when the time came, Steve would not be able to deal with planning my funeral. I intended to pre-plan and prepay for everything so that he would not have to worry about a thing.

I wanted this event, my final hurrah, to be as joyous as my life had been. I wanted my guests to be served hot fudge sundaes. My whole adult life I had battled a sluggish metabolism. I stayed away from Heggy's. Hot fudge sundaes were forbidden fruit I could never have. Now, I saw them as a celebration of life, the joy of living for the moment, and the need to leave the world without regrets, with a maraschino cherry on top. I wanted to impart this invaluable lesson as my last official act on Earth.

I started hunting for the music I wanted played at my funeral. "Someday," by blues belter Michelle Willson, brought me to tears, but it was too sad. I wanted people to celebrate my life, not roll in the aisles wailing.

I tried Josh Groban instead. His sweet baritone was probably played at more funerals than "Taps." Hearing her favorite singer, Dillie pushed open the door and came in to listen, laying her head on my lap.

I stroked her beautiful face and cried. "I will miss you so much, Dillie," I told her. "Please take care of your daddy for me."

Dillie licked my tears, enjoying the salt. Her tongue flipped out of the side of her mouth in the goofy way it always did, which made me smile.

Pets are completely in tune with their human companions. They know when we are happy or afraid. They know when our world is crumbling around us. Dillie lay down at my feet next to Lady. A few minutes later, Spazz the cat joined us.

Next, I decided to write my obituary, not because I am a control freak and not because no one else could, but because I felt an overwhelming need to put my life on paper. I needed to see that I had left a mark.

When I left this Earth, no one would know I had even been here. I planned to be cremated and have my ashes scattered with Steve's someday on our land in Idaho. I wasn't even going to have a headstone. There wouldn't be a granite marker telling the world that Melanie Butera had been a vet and a loving person.

As I struggled to find the words to describe my life, Pavarotti began to sing "*E lucevan le stelle*," the heartbreaking aria from *Tosca*. Pavarotti's rendition is the most beautiful three minutes of anguish I have ever heard. The aria demolished me. I wept uncontrollably and finally allowed myself to have the breakdown I had held at bay.

"Is this all there is?" I said out loud to a Creator I thought would not answer me. "I'm just here, and then *poof*, I'm gone? Did I do anything that will last?"

Cancer had taken *Il Maestro's* life, too, but his gift and voice were immortal. What had I done? I had been a good vet, but my work would not endure.

When I had no more tears to cry, I reached down to stroke Dillie's head. I thought about the day she'd come to the clinic, how fragile her life had been. Then I thought about the thousands of letters of love we had received about Dillie. I had saved her. And now she affected more lives than I could if I worked as a vet for a hundred years.

I trashed the draft of my obituary and found a file I had entitled "Dillie." It was the first draft of a book I had begun to write about Dillie two years earlier. When she became a celebrity in 2010, people were writing about her and relating her story. I had thought at the time, *I know Dillie better than anyone. I should write a book about her.* As I reread the pages I had written before my cancer, before Pat's cancer, before Dean's tragic fall, before all the losses of the animals and people in my life that had occurred in the past two years, I knew I had to finish this book. Even if it never sold a copy, even if no one else ever read it, I had to finish it. This was my legacy. This was my granite marker. This was my proof that I had existed.

With the sun rising, and Dillie, Lady, and Spazz lounging around me, I began to put my affairs in order.

I started to write *Dillie the Deer: Love on Hooves.*

Chapter 32

Blessed Are the Mournful

My childhood memories of Christmas Eve are magical. I can recall the glittering Christmas tree with all the beautiful presents underneath, and my brother, sisters, and me racing to open our presents after midnight Mass. Mom and Grandma Rose had been cooking the entire day, and the house was filled with the rich smell of *sugo*, spaghetti sauce. Platters of homemade Sicilian sweets—*pizzelles*, cannoli, *torrone*—adorned the tables. In the oven, the top layer of mozzarella was bubbling away on the lasagna. No matter how many dishes they had cooked, there was always lasagna.

Christmas Eve 2012, my fifty-second, was not magical. Steve and I had stopped putting up a tree years ago, because Dillie inevitably knocked it over. Though my mother was having her annual party, which would surely involve lasagna, it was not going to be the same. Grandma Rose had passed two years prior. My radiation oncologist had planned my holiday. I was to spend the morning getting a biopsy on the mass the surgeon had found.

Steve dropped me off that Christmas Eve morning at the hospital. I didn't want him hanging around all day, worried and impatient. It was a cold, gray, dreary, rainy day. The weather fit my mood.

My procedure began on a familiar CT table. They were going to take some scans, then do the biopsy while I was still on the table. As I lay there with my arms up over my head, the technician spoke to me through the speaker in the machine.

"Hold your breath. . . . Okay, now exhale. . . . Now, deep breath." Partway through the scan, she threw me a curveball. "Now, breathe. . . . Okay, exhale. . . . Do you have a deer that lives in your house?"

I would have preferred being known for my professional skills, but my reputation as a locally famous Internet kook did give me an occasional laugh.

The doctor and the nurse came in to begin the biopsy. The doctor explained that he was going to do a local block and then go in and grab some tissue. I had done thousands of needle aspirates and ultrasound-guided deep biopsies in my career. The animals had never complained. I sometimes thought it was my karma to have all the painful things I had done to my patients done to me while I was ill. This biopsy supported my theory—the pain was so intense that even thoughts of Dean and Pat couldn't dispel it. I could not escape this pain.

"Don't move!" the nurse said.

My eyes were still closed, but I could feel my shoulders being held down against the table. I realized I was in the CT machine. Inside the tube. The lower half of my body, where they were doing the biopsy, was outside the machine. I wondered how the nurse could be holding down my shoulders. I peeked over each shoulder to confirm I was enclosed in the machine. Although it was physically impossible for anyone to stand behind me, I felt my shoulders being steadily pressed to the table.

While I was preoccupied with the mystery, the doctor finished the biopsy. "Okay, we're done," he said.

The invisible hands released their grip on my shoulders.

The team moved me to a recovery area where Janet, the solitary nurse on duty, instructed me to choose any bed or chair I wanted. I was the only patient there.

I settled into a comfy chair in the corner, and the nurse took my vital signs. She told me she would have to check my vitals every ten minutes for an hour before I could leave. I started listening to Christmas music on my headphones, but since I was the only one in the room, I pulled out the headphones and let the music play aloud.

I thought again about the pressure on my shoulders. I couldn't help wondering if Dean, Pat, Grandma Rose, or an angel had been there to help me. Nothing that mystical had ever happened to me before. I knew my visits with Dean and Pat during my radiation treatments were a psychological escape hatch. I never believed they were really there. But what had just happened on the CT table seemed completely real.

Janet came in again to check my vitals. She was polite but not chatty. As she left the room, she stopped and took out a small card from her scrub pocket, read it, and then replaced it. She looked at the time and left the room.

I called Steve to tell him that I should be good to go in a half hour. "We have to stop at the clinic on the way home," he told me. "The fish have to be fed."

Steve, much to the exasperation of my entire staff, is obsessive about the aquarium in our clinic's lobby. He had named all the fish, and one of them, Ernie, ate right from his fingertips. I protested. I had too much to do that afternoon to bother with the fish, I was still in pain from the biopsy, and I was exhausted. We had presents to wrap and food to pack into the car, and we had to be at Mom's by six. "Just go feed the fish now," I told him, "and then come pick me up."

Janet came to take the last readings for the hour. My blood pressure had held steady, so I was able to leave. I gathered up my coat and scarf. As I did, the phone rang. Janet answered it and, after a few words with the caller, raised her hand, gesturing for me to stop.

"Sorry," she explained. "That was the doctor. He's concerned about the amount of bleeding during the biopsy. He wants you to stay another three hours."

Three hours! I would not even have time to shower before Steve and I were expected for dinner. But I settled back into my chair without complaining. I called Steve to tell him not to pick me up. He did enough complaining for both of us.

"It's Christmas Eve! Don't they know you have things

to do?" he said. He was grumpy about having to do all my chores to get ready for the night. We would have to go right from the hospital to the party.

"Don't forget," he said. "We have to stop at the clinic and feed the fish."

I sighed and said good-bye.

When Janet came in to take my vitals again, I thanked her for working on a holiday.

"Oh, that's okay," she answered, surprised by my gratitude. "I can't be home during the holidays anyway." She didn't elaborate and retreated to her desk. She took out the card that was in her scrubs pocket and read it again. I noticed she was trying unsuccessfully to keep from crying. She brushed away a few escaped tears.

I was so absorbed by my own problems I hadn't noticed how sad she was. Despite her aura of grief, she was trying to do her job and be as pleasant as she could.

"Are you okay?" I asked.

Janet apologized. "Holidays are hard," she answered. "I lost my son last year."

I murmured something sympathetic, and she pulled the card from her scrub pocket. On the front was a photo of a handsome young man, fit and smiling.

On the back of the photo was a handwritten Bible verse, and Janet read it aloud to me, "Blessed are the mournful, for they shall be comforted."

"He's so young," I said.

"Twenty-one."

"Was it a car accident?" I'm not sure why I chose to ask for details. It was probably rude, but I felt she needed to talk.

"He was murdered," Janet answered, and her tears fell. She looked at the card and read the verse aloud again. "Blessed are the mournful, for they shall be comforted."

"Losing a child is bad enough," I commented, "but losing one to murder . . . I don't know how anyone can ever get over that."

"You can't, but I'm working on it."

She went on to tell me that after her son's death, she had lost her faith in God. She could not understand how the merciful God she had been raised to trust could allow a young man with so much promise to be murdered. She had fallen into a deep hole of despair and was struggling to climb out.

"You must feel the same way," she said, knowing the severity of my diagnosis.

Though I had not spoken to anyone about my doubts, I had been questioning my beliefs since my diagnosis. I confessed to Janet, a stranger, the cracks in my own faith. I had not yet revealed my doubts to anyone.

I told her I know people who have so much faith in God that they could step off a cliff and trust that God would provide a bridge for them. My faith was not that strong. I was a scientist. I was educated in the laws of physics, chemistry, and biology. Although I had knelt in a pew in a Catholic church when I was a child, I had stopped attending church as an adult. The scientist in me knew deep down that a caring and loving God was not possible. How could He be? The laws of thermodynamics could not measure Him. His electron orbitals could not be predicted. His Krebs cycle could not be charted. Immortality, eternity, and deity were concepts that science could never prove, and therefore, they did not exist.

I had come to the conclusion that my cancer had returned so that I could rid myself of those doubts. The cure I
was meant to find was not a cure for my cancer. My doubt-
ing, scientific mind still needed healing. After my diagnosis, I started going to the local Catholic church.

"I know that crevasse," Janet said as she took my vitals.
"There is no bridge."

She sat in the chair next to mine. "But you know what?"
she said, with more of a smile than I had seen from her all
morning. "Things happened. So many things . . . so many
coincidences that I started to realize they weren't coincidences after all. I realized they were the bricks God was
laying for me to lead me out of grief.

"Everywhere I go," she explained, "I meet mothers
grieving for their sons. We help each other. I meet them
here at the hospital, in church, even on vacation. My husband and I took our first trip since it happened. I didn't
want to go, but our loss strained our marriage, and we were
trying to repair the damage. We were in the Caribbean and
shared a cab with strangers, a couple from Iowa. The wife
and I began to talk. It turned out that they were on vacation
for the same reason we were. Their son had died of cancer the same week our Thomas died. By the end of the cab
ride, we prayed together and for each other. We still keep
in touch. The two of us are bonded by our grief, but also by
hope for better days. 'Blessed are the mournful . . . '"

I thought about what had happened on the scan table
that morning. *Was this a sign? Could my scientific mind be
wrong? Was there a bridge under my feet even though I could
not see, feel, or measure it?*

When there were only a few minutes left in my three-hour sentence, I called Steve and told him to come pick me up.

"Don't forget, we have to feed the fish," he said.

I had learned to let Steve do what he wanted when he was obsessed with something, even if it made no sense. He could have fed those fish anytime that day. The clinic was far from my mother's house, but there would be no living with Steve until Ernie got his fish flakes.

"Whatever," I said with resignation, forgetting our holiday timetable.

Janet came back in and started to disconnect me from the monitors. "You're good," she said.

I hugged her. "God bless you on your path." A blessing seemed appropriate.

"You, too," she answered. "Don't worry, and don't lose your faith."

With perfect timing, Steve pulled up to the valet station just as I reached the front door. Instead of getting on the freeway, the fastest route to my mother's, he took the rural road that led us to the clinic and the hungry fish.

I didn't know how to express what had happened to me. It had become a transformative, magical Christmas Eve.

When we got to the clinic, he insisted I come inside. I was still in a lot of pain, and the painkillers they had given me were making me queasy. "Can't you just go in and feed them without me?" I protested.

"No, you have to come in."

I staggered into the lobby. Before me was a glittering Christmas tree. Beneath it were wrapped presents addressed to Steve, Lady, Dillie, Spazz, and me. Each bough of the beautiful tree was hung with handmade ornaments containing photographs of my patients in tiny ornate frames. An inscription was on the back of each one.

"Thank you for saving my life, Dr. B!" It was from a dog who had been hit by a car, whose ruptured diaphragm I had repaired.

"Thank you, Doc, for putting me back together." That was from Ginger, the dachshund.

It took me several days to read all the heartfelt messages. At the moment, all I could do was cry.

Steve hugged me. "So many people love you," he said. "And all these animals depend on you. You have to get well."

When we got home late that night, we were greeted at the door by our own hungry animals. Steve insisted I go sit down. As I curled up on the living room couch with a blanket, he tended to the grumbling stomachs, including all four of Dillie's. Eventually, Steve joined me and turned on the television. He flipped through several guy movies like *Rambo*, *Con Air*, and something starring the Rock. He settled on the movie *King of Kings*.

Since I have known Steve, he has never been religious. He believes in God but doesn't affiliate himself with any church and is impatient with my Catholic traditions. For him to choose a movie about the life of Jesus, even on Christmas Eve, over a selection of macho fare, was inexplicable. When we tuned in, the scene was the Sermon on the Mount. The first words Jesus spoke were:

"Blessed are the mournful, for they shall
be comforted."

Chapter 33

Hope Was Here to Stay

I spent the rest of that holiday weekend obeying my surgeon and getting my affairs in order. It was a luxury for me not to be at the office. I wanted to get as much done as I could.

I was still wrestling with my skeptical scientist side. I had reached out to a Catholic priest, but his rote statements about God's grace didn't seem to have much to do with my situation. I took a break from writing and getting our house in order to call my friend Don.

Don and I have been close since we were teenagers working at a Baskin-Robbins. We had deep philosophical discussions over the Pralines 'n Cream. Don was now a nondenominational Christian minister, so I called him up.

We talked for a long time, but Don's explanation was

very simple. I had a human mind, which was limited by nature. God's mind did not have limits. We humans are like ants, staring up at a starry sky. The ant sees the sky and the stars, and knows they exist, but lacks the capacity to understand the cosmos. Actual ants and most other animals accept this, but human arrogance makes us believe that we can understand the universe. We cannot. Divinity is beyond our comprehension. Accepting that God exists, although we can never fully understand Him, is the ultimate test of faith.

My scientific skepticism was an obstruction to my faith. Believing in the irrational was the ultimate test. God existed whether I could quantify Him or not, and He was trying to get my attention. He held down my shoulders on the CT table and introduced me to other souls walking the same path.

I went back to the hospital on New Year's Eve to have my Mediport placed. The device was being implanted in my shoulder vein to allow the chemo doctor to flood my body with caustic drugs without scarring my veins. The port was to stay in until I was five years cancer-free.

I didn't see Janet on New Year's Eve. The nurse that night told me she was off for the weekend. I was disappointed, because I wanted to tell her how much our conversation had moved me.

The radiology intervention department was busier than it had been on Christmas Eve. The receptionist gave me a restaurant-style pager and had me wait until the crew was ready for me. After parking the car, Steve joined me in the small waiting area. The room was feebly decorated for the holidays, but the staff was friendly and warm.

I pulled up Dillie's webcam on my tablet. She was sleeping soundly on her bed, rocking her head back and forth, wiggling her ears. Lady was lying in front of her and as we watched, Spazz snuck into the room and jumped on the bed, snuggling in next to Dillie. Both Steve and I smiled, understanding the peace our little group brought people across the globe.

My pager started buzzing and blinking. It was time for my procedure.

I was shown to a dressing room and given a gown and a pair of hospital-issue socks. A tall, athletic-looking woman in green scrubs came in and introduced herself.

"Hi," she said. "I'm the nurse practitioner, and I'll be placing your port today. My name is Pat."

I smiled. After asking me a few questions about my medical history, off she went.

Then a man in scrubs came in. "Hi," he said. "I'm the nurse anesthetist, and I will be monitoring your vital signs. My name is Dean."

So Pat and Dean were there for me. My eyes stung.

Seeing my tears, nurse anesthetist Dean tried to calm me. "Oh, honey," he said. "This won't hurt. Don't be afraid."

I couldn't tell him the real reason for my tears. I wasn't afraid at all. I knew I would be fine. I was under the protection of my friends.

By the time I met my chemo doctor during the first week of the New Year, my hope was as fragile as a sickly, newborn fawn. Despite the mysterious and powerful events I had experienced, I had no expectation that I was going to live. I believed that God was making Himself known to me, but only to call me home and to ease my fear about the journey.

Within minutes of my new doctor's friendly greeting, he told me, "You have a choice. If you go ahead with chemo, we start next week."

"What's my other choice?" I asked, thinking he was going to suggest some experimental therapy or radiation.

"Your other choice," he said, "is to enjoy the time you have left without the medication making you sicker."

"That's not a choice at all," I said.

"It's going to be tough," he said.

"So am I." I was all in.

"You're going to have to take some time off from work," he told me.

That wasn't likely, but I promised him I would get as much rest as I could. In the lobby, Steve asked, "What did he say?"

I put on my winter coat and forced a smile. "Don't worry," I said. "Everything's going to be good. It's all about the chemo."

Shortly after I started chemotherapy, my mother called me and said, "I want you to go to a service with me. There's going to be a doctor there with great healing powers. His name is Dr. Nemeh."

Months earlier, my friend Sandy had been suffering from a mysterious neurological ailment that made her dizzy whenever she moved. Neurologists couldn't determine what the disease was and dismissed it as psychosomatic. Instead of giving up, Sandy had returned to Ohio to see Issam Nemeh, a Cleveland-area cardiologist who had an international reputation as a gifted spiritual healer. Dr. Nemeh had not only diagnosed her on the spot but also had corrected her problem by performing spinal manipulation and electroacupuncture.

I had never heard of Dr. Nemeh before Sandy told me about him, but I was grateful that he had cured my friend. Sandy described him as a modest man of God, not like the flamboyant "faith healers" of televangelism fame.

I was still skeptical, but I obliged my mother, because I would do anything to bolster her hope that I could survive.

The following weekend, Mom and I waited among hundreds of people to see Dr. Nemeh. He was just as my friend Sandy had said: unassuming, meek, and humble. This was a service. There were no TV cameras, bands playing, or speaking in tongues. A simple, quiet man approached the microphone and told us he was Dr. Nemeh. He was a classically trained cardiologist, he explained, but throughout his life he had known the healing power of the Holy Spirit. He knew that there was more to medicine than the quality of the doctor and the drugs. He had witnessed miracles, but he also knew some patients would not be cured, he said, "at least in this realm." Sometimes, he told us, the cure helps not the physical body but the spirit.

After a long wait, my mother and I received our blessing from Dr. Nemeh. I have been in places in which the power of the Holy Spirit was as obvious as the North Star. When my mother and I stood in front of the Shroud of

Turin in Torino, Italy, I felt that type of presence. When we saw Mother Teresa speak at a local college a few years before she died, I felt it then, too. Dr. Nemeh had that blessed aura. When he touched my mother, she fainted.

My mother was determined for Dr. Nemeh to see me as a patient. Knowing Sandy helped us skip the six-week waiting list—I saw Dr. Nemeh at his medical office the evening after my mother called. Among the portraits of saints that hung on his office wall, I noticed Padre Pio above his desk. The Vatican has since canonized Padro Pio, an Italian priest and stigmatic who died in 1968. Many miracles had been attributed to him before and after his death. I had purchased a medallion of the padre more than a decade earlier.

My visit to Dr. Nemeh was three days after my first chemo, when the chemo demons were returning to possess me. The fatigue, queasiness, and pain were just starting. They would intensify during the next week and gradually subside. Just when my energy started to come back and food no longer tasted like copper pipe, it was time for another round.

That night, I was feeling shaky and sick. From the moment Dr. Nemeh came into the exam room, I felt calm and tranquil. He introduced himself. Up close, he was the same quiet, unassuming man I had met at the prayer service, but his personal presence was even more powerful. He radiated kindness and love.

He asked about my cancer as he conducted the medical exam. Then he began electroacupuncture with a set of electric leads and a laptop. I had faith in Dr. Nemeh's spiritual powers because he had cured Sandy, but I was there to seek his counsel about faith. During the acupuncture, I talked to him about the conflict I had as a scientist believing completely in the improbable existence of a God. Had he ever had doubts?

"No, never," he answered quietly. "I have felt His presence. I have seen His work. He is very real."

When Dr. Nemeh had finished the procedure, he gave me the best medicine I received during my entire cancer treatment: hope. He was the first doctor to give me the hope I needed to fight the battle of my life.

"You are going to be fine," he said. "The angels around you are there to help you. They aren't taking you home."

I did not expect a miracle cure from Dr. Nemeh. He was a faith healer to me in the most literal sense—he healed my broken faith.

I poured myself into finishing Dillie's book. Everywhere I went, *Dillie the Deer* went with me. I worked on it every second I could: rising early, staying up late, between patients, in doctors' waiting rooms, and waiting for my lunch at the only Thai restaurant in town. I was so focused on writing that I wasn't absorbing what I was saying. Right in front of me, in my own handwriting, were the answers to all my struggles. I just didn't realize it.

On the night I wrote the last line of my manuscript, Dillie and Lady sat next to me in my office. I felt a great sense of accomplishment and wanted to tell someone. Steve was in bed, so the only ones who heard my triumphant "I did it!" were the furry subjects of my book. Lady looked up curiously, and Dillie kept chewing her cud.

Relishing my small victory, I climbed into bed. Whether

the manuscript was published or not, it was finished. Even if no one else ever read it, I had written something that showed I existed.

The e-mail alert on my phone buzzed. Normally, I would have ignored any message until morning, but I just happened to glance over and see it was from a doctor. Thinking the message might be from a colleague, I grabbed my phone to read it.

Dr. Butera,

My wife, Barbara, is losing hope in her battle with a progressive disease. She lives to see the deer that come to our backyard. She has loved Dillie from the first time she saw her. I would love to give Barbara a present she would cherish forever. Any chance we could visit?

With hope,
Dr. Allen S.

I called Allen and learned that Barbara had mitochondrial disease.

"She is losing hope," he said. "She's tired of fighting her body."

How could I possibly refuse? I talked with Allen about my current battle with cancer and my struggle to keep my own hope alive. He generously offered any assistance he could provide.

"I work at the Cleveland Clinic with some of the best oncologists in the world," he told me. "If you need an introduction or even a ride there, I would be happy to help."

A few nights later, his wife e-mailed me:

The simple reality is that my journey on Earth should have ended some time ago. All traditional and experimental treatment options failed. In the absence of medical hope, I have reinvented my own version, over and over again. Perhaps I was meant to find hope in Dillie or maybe we were meant to bring you a dose of the hope, support, and love you have clearly given to so many.

Barbara's battle had been so much longer and harder than mine. I had no right to lose hope and let myself die.

Dillie ambled into my office and laid her head on my lap. She was the physical incarnation of hope and love for so many people all over the world, and now she was bringing me that hope, too.

I stroked her pretty face, and her long pink tongue flipped out the side of her mouth and stayed there. I laughed and kissed her on the nose.

"Dillie," I told her, "I am not going to cry any more. I am going to be just fine."

She gave me another slurp and folded her legs to lie down. She wasn't going anywhere.

Hope was here to stay.

Chapter 34

~~~~~~~~~

The Rainbow Bridge

At age seventeen, our beloved dog Lady was facing her own end-of-life issues. The nerves in her legs were deteriorating, and her liver was shutting down. Although I had promised Lady at the beginning of my chemo that we would be there for each other to the end, her condition was worsening rapidly. I knew I would not be able to keep my promise.

By early spring of 2013, Lady could no longer climb on the bed with Dillie. She was often bewildered, could barely hear, and her legs were losing strength.

"It's time," Steve kept telling me.

I protested. Not now. I couldn't bear to think of euthanizing Lady, but I knew I would soon have to.

Lady was only five when we had first moved into the

gray house on the hill. Steve played a game with her every day. He would let her out of the truck at the end of the driveway when he arrived home. She raced him up the quarter mile to the house, black curly ears flapping in the wind as she galloped. She always won, but it wasn't because of her speed. Her intelligence carried the day. She figured out a shortcut. Instead of running the curves of the driveway, she ran through the woods and made a straight line to the house.

Steve laughed as he watched her leap through the woods. Lady loved this game. She threw her entire heart into every step, beating Steve every time. She greeted him at the back door, jubilant in victory.

Now, Lady seemed to be aging all at once. Dillie appeared to sense the changes in her best friend. Sometimes when Lady could not climb on the bed, Dillie lay down next to her on the floor. Every time Lady's unsteady legs made her stumble and fall down the stairs, Dillie rushed to her side.

One afternoon in April, Dillie was lounging on her bed, with Lady asleep on the floor nearby. I was just a few steps away in my upstairs office. I heard the repetitive thuds that I recognized as the sound of an animal having a seizure. I ran next door to find Lady convulsing.

Dillie jumped off the bed and stood over Lady. Her best friend's trembling body was completely within Dillie's four-hooved stance. Dillie stood guard, licking and comforting Lady. She nursed her for the few seconds the seizure lasted, and then for the five minutes needed for Lady to regain her composure.

Lady had a spinal condition known as degenerative myelopathy, which was causing her to lose nerve sensation to her limbs. Her liver no longer functioned well. Her entire body was shutting down. I could not cure her condition. I did what I could, but I knew she didn't have much time left. I could not give her more time.

A few weeks after the seizure, I was cleaning out an old filing cabinet and came across a file with Lady's papers in it. Steve and I had adopted Lady when she was two years old from a loving family who felt they could not provide her with the attention she demanded. In a file, I found Lady's original AKC papers saying her full name was "Lady Chardonnay" and giving the name of her previous owner, which I had long since forgotten. I soon tracked down a current address and e-mail.

I sent an e-mail letting them know what a joy she had been to us, how much she was loved, and what a great life she had.

More than a dozen years ago, we adopted a standard poodle from you named Lady. I just wanted to let you know what a precious dog she has been to us all these years. Unfortunately, she has aged dramatically in this last year. She is nearly seventeen years old now, and I'm afraid the end is near.

Lady has been a treasured part of our family all these years, and she has become renowned as the sister to our deer, Dillie, who is known all over the world through her webcam. You can see pictures of Lady with Dillie on our website. Lady traveled with us to Oregon and all the way to the Florida Keys. She camped out in the woods with us in Idaho and rode in an airboat in the Everglades. She even got a police warning once for chasing a rooster on the streets of Key West, where the roosters are "protected citizens." She used to go to work with me every day at the veterinary clinic. She helped us raise not only Dillie but also many of the critters in our house. Along with Dillie, Lady has touched people's lives all over the world. She even gets mail from schoolchildren in South Korea and Brazil.

She has led a good life, and she has been cherished.

I will always consider Lady the best dog I have ever had. I cannot bear the thought of losing her. When the time comes, I have to do what is best for her and not what spares me heartache.

Thank you for sharing her with us, and very best wishes.

I suspected a dog as good as Lady had to have made a lasting impression on their hearts. To my delight, Lady's previous family answered me warmly and asked me to share their love with her.

By the end of spring, I knew it was time. Lady, who lived for visitors, searching for toys to bring them, did not even lift up her head anymore when people arrived. Her falls down the stairs were becoming more frequent and dangerous. We had taken her twin-bed mattress off its frame in our room and set it on the floor for her, but she could no longer even get on the mattress without help. I was not going to be able to wait until I finished chemo. It was time. It was no easier for me to make this decision than it is for any of my clients.

I brought home the necessities: the clipper, a stethoscope, a sedative, and the euthanasia solution. My plan was to give Lady the injection on the front porch lying on her favorite bed, surrounded by her stuffed toys. Steve suggested I ask my colleague Stacy to give the injection, but I knew this was the right thing to do, and that I could do it.

How many animals had I put down during my career? I couldn't even count. Maybe as many as 10,000. Maybe more. I was confident I could perform this final act of kindness, as I often told myself it was, for our beloved girl.

On a Sunday afternoon on a beautiful spring day, I sedated Lady on the front porch and let her fall asleep on her bed. I didn't want Dillie to see what I was doing, and Steve did not want to be there. He was supposed to keep Dillie busy in the house while I finished the dreaded task. A phone call took him away from his duty. Dillie found a way through the front door, which was open a crack for the clippers' electrical cord. She walked out onto the front porch just as I was clipping Lady's hair over her vein for the final injection.

Dillie stood over Lady, sedated and asleep, and licked her face. Then she turned around and went back into the house. She had said good-bye.

Serenaded by songbirds in the yard she had called home for more than a decade, our beloved Lady passed away.

I had overestimated my ability to detach myself from

the situation. I sat over my dear friend Lady and bawled like a child.

"Oh, Lady," I said. "I am so sorry."

Steve came out just then. "It's done?" he asked.

I nodded. "You were right, I should have had Stacy do it," I said. "How could I do this to my own dog?"

"You did the right thing," he said. "She couldn't go on the way she was."

I looked at Lady's lifeless body and sobbed. We had been through so much together. I thought about how she would not leave my side after my first cancer surgery. I re-called how when the chemo made me sick and I was hud-dled under blankets, aching, she would be right next to me, laying her head on my arm.

Steve pulled me up and hugged me. "There's worse things than dying," he said. "She's at peace now."

These were the very words I used countless times to console clients in similar circumstances. I knew it was true, but those words didn't stop the pain.

"Go inside," he said. "I'll take care of her."

He buried her out in the yard near Neffie and Screamie. The day did an Ohio weather one-eighty. The sun disappeared, and a downpour began. The rain continued off and on.

When Dillie went outside for her usual four p.m. ex-ercise, the sun was out again. On any other day, she would have grazed around the yard and wooded areas. Instead, she made her way directly to Lady's grave. Steve went out to get her to follow him to the barn for the daily walk, but she wouldn't move. He couldn't even get her to follow him to her favorite wild rose patch.

She stood on Lady's grave for hours. The rain came and went, and she remained. By eight o'clock that night, I could stand it no more.

"You have to go out and get her," I told Steve.

Steve wiped away his tears and went to comfort his grieving girl. "I know you loved Lady, Dillie," he told her. "But she doesn't hurt anymore. She's free now."

Dillie licked his face and followed her daddy back home.

Dillie's heart was broken, just as ours were, and she grieved the loss of her poodle sister for days. Each day that week, she would not go anywhere in the yard until she had visited Lady's grave. After standing there with her head lowered for ten minutes or more, she continued her usual exercise routine and headed for the wild roses.

I didn't have the heart to visit the grave for a month. Steve urged me to, but I just couldn't. I had ordered a granite marker embellished with a laser-etched picture of Lady. When it arrived, I made my first visit with Steve and Dillie. Spazz came lumbering behind. The entire family was there as we said another good-bye.

I thought of the anonymously written essay about the timeless bond between animals and the people who love them, which we send to our clients in sympathy when they lose a pet. When pets die, the piece explains, they go to the Rainbow Bridge just this side of heaven. The animals play together, happy and content, and are restored to the way they were in their prime. They wait for those they love to join them, greet them joyously, and cross over the Rainbow Bridge with their special human friends, never to be separated again.

"Thank you, Lady," I said. "We will miss you forever. Wait for me at the Rainbow Bridge."

I placed the marker on Lady's grave. It had an inscription. The saying was just a standard selection, a greeting-card verse supplied by the marker company, but the words rang true:

> If love could have saved you, you would have
> lived forever.

Chapter 35

Solving a Mystery Disease

I had just completed my tenth round of chemo and felt as if I was down for the count. The chemo demons had been busy. All my muscles ached, even the little ones around my eyes. My mouth and throat were on fire. Although my feet and fingertips were numb, they felt like someone was using me as a voodoo doll. I was one day shy of my fifty-third birthday, and I looked and felt 200. I might have been ghostly pale and have had a cue ball head, but I hoped I was in store for some good news. I had had PET scans the previous week and was awaiting a call from the oncologist. If the scans were negative, if no cancer lit up on them, I was done with chemo, at least for a while.

"We never say cure," Cathy, my chemo nurse, told me. "We only hope for remission."

My patients didn't care how I looked. They needed me. No matter how I felt, I had a cat in the hospital in renal failure and a full day of appointments. I got ready for work.

I got through my morning appointments by sheer determination. I dragged myself back to my comfy office chair and skipped lunch, trying not to let my staff know how terrible I felt. As I sat hunched over in my chair, racked with pain and shivering from the chills, my technicians, Jessica and Noel, brought me a blanket and tried to make me comfortable. Our receptionist, Joelle, came in with a steaming cup of vanilla chai and Advil.

Jessica knocked on the door and apologized for disturbing me. She told me we had an emergency.

She ushered me in to see Wrigly, a four-year-old black Lab lying on a mat in the treatment area. "He looks as if he's in shock," she said, "so we brought him right to the back."

The dog's gums didn't look pale, as I would expect with a shock patient. He didn't even lift his head when I started my exam. He was profoundly weak. He had a rapid heart rate: 250 beats per minute. For a dog as large as Wrigly, that was extremely high. Since usually only dogs with cardiac arrhythmias have rates that fast, I put the ECG on him while Jess prepped him for an IV. His heartbeat was not irregular. His temperature was 104.5, two degrees above normal, which was not high enough for heatstroke and unusual for a hypothermic, shocky dog.

The owner said Wrigly had been fine the day before, just straining a little when he defecated. Whatever was hitting him, it was fast. We threw an IV catheter in him and started rapid IV fluids.

He seemed to have pain in his belly, so we moved him to the X-ray table for films. Some of the things that could drop an otherwise healthy dog in just a few hours would show up on an X-ray. We were looking for a ruptured abdominal tumor, a perforated bowel, or stomach/bowel torsion, any explanation for why this dog who was healthy less than a day ago was dying in front of our eyes.

As Jess and Noel positioned Wrigly for films, they noticed something odd. "There's some kind of fluid coming out of his gums," Jess said.

"Drool?" I asked.

"No," Jess said, "it's sticky. Like plasma." She showed me some on her fingers. "And it smells like blood."

"It's got to be drool," I said. "What else could it be?"

Noel, whom I had nicknamed "Gerbil" because of her tiny four-foot-nine-inch frame and boundless energy, was never shy about grabbing my attention when she felt I was not listening to her or the others. "No. We know drool," she insisted. "We get it on us all the time. This is not drool."

"From his rectum, too," Jess added. "The same fluid. It's clear, but smells like blood."

Wrigly's slightly labored breaths smelled the same way.

Joelle rushed in to grab a gurney. "We have another emergency," she announced.

Noel went out with Joelle to get the next emergency to the back. They carried in a dog who could have been Wrigly's twin, a black Lab also lying on its side, breathing hard.

"Guess what," Noel said. "This one also has fluid that smells like blood coming out of her gums."

The second dog, Bella, also had a fever, a whopping heart rate in the mid-200s, and was shocky, but she had bright red gums. Blood-tinged fluid dribbled out of her rectum.

I had seen a lot of crazy symptoms, but I had never seen a dog leaching plasma out of every orifice. Now, I had two look-alike patients with the exact same never-before-seen symptoms. Something was going on. I felt as if we were in the hot zone.

"This has to be some kind of septic shock," I said. It was the one type of shock that would make the gums red, not pale or muddy. "Do these two owners know each other? Have the dogs been together at all?"

Joelle shook her head. "The owners are sitting next to each other in the lobby, but they don't seem to know each other. I'll go out and talk to them."

"Find out as much as you can about where the dogs have been or what they might have been exposed to."

As we placed the IV in Bella and started her fluids, I could hear the conversation between the clients and Joelle. No, they didn't know each other, they hadn't been anywhere in common. Wrigly had just gotten back from a trip to Cincinnati and hadn't even been in town this past week.

A third client, who had come to the clinic to pick up some medication overheard the conversation and chimed in. "Cincinnati? I just heard on the news there was some kind of dog disease there. Some type of kennel cough that is killing dogs."

I knew that kennel cough doesn't kill dogs and assumed the client was mistaken. I ran to my computer and Googled "dog disease Cincinnati," and there it was. Four dogs who had been at the same boarding facility had come down with a mysterious illness and had died within twenty-four hours.

The emergency clinicians there had described the disease as HGE, or hemorrhagic gastroenteritis, in other words, bloody inflamed bowel. I had treated thousands of HGE cases, and the condition was rarely fatal. HGE patients had bloody stool, but not one I had treated had a super high heart rate, a fever, or fluid leaching out from the gums. I was not looking at HGE with these two Labs.

The online article mentioned that the Ohio Department of Agriculture was investigating the disease. While the staff did blood work and X-rays on our twin mystery patients, I called the state veterinarian.

"I'm wondering about these dogs in Cincy," I said after introducing myself.

"Well," he said, "the truth is there were actually twelve dogs, not four, that had been at that boarding facility and got sick. All but one died, despite aggressive treatment. Some of them have bloody stool, but most have rectal bleeding. They show signs of vasculitis, oozing plasma from injured blood vessels, which leaks from their gums, rectums, and noses."

The state veterinarian continued to describe my patients as if he were right here with us. "Their breath smells like blood. They develop fluid in the abdomen and in or around the lungs. Most of them developed neurologic signs and seizured before they died. They have the classic MERS and SARS response of septic shock."

"This is like Ebola!" I said.

"Don't say that aloud," he responded. "People will panic. But we do believe this organism is acting very much by the same biological mechanisms that Ebola does. We believe it's the canine circovirus."

"The what?" I had never heard of that virus.

He explained that based on work done very recently on similar cases at the University of California, they believed it was actually a swine virus that had jumped species. Postmortem results on the California and Cincinnati dogs were similar. Toxins and more common diseases had been ruled out in the Cincinnati dogs. They had even tested for the known hemorrhagic fevers of deer and horses.

"Oh, and I forgot to mention," he continued. "If the dogs get through this, they may slough damaged skin tissue."

This statement set off major alarm bells. I was treating a dog who was sloughing tissue off its entire back. We had biopsied the area, and it had been read as "vasculitis of undetermined origin." I had seen another dog earlier that week who had had the fever, weakness, and rapid heart rate, but it had responded to treatment with fluids and antibiotics.

"I think I have four cases of this," I told the state vet. "Two here right now looking like septic shock and oozing fluid everywhere. One earlier in the week who wasn't quite as bad and got better, and one who is sloughing the skin on her back. One of these dogs just got back from Cincinnati."

"Hmm," he said. "Interesting. Can you find out when they were there? Also, any way you can send us stool and blood on all four? If any pass away, we need tissue specimens."

"Absolutely," I said. "Is this contagious dog to dog? Dog to human?"

"We don't know yet," he said. "We recommend using isolation protocols just in case. It spread like wildfire through that boarding facility in Cincy."

The X-rays and blood work on both dogs looked much better than the dogs did themselves. Despite the fluids and antibiotics, their condition was deteriorating.

I started reading articles on MERS, SARS, Ebola, and other hemorrhagic fevers. I reasoned that understanding the mechanisms of these viruses would help me figure out a treatment. I took a crash refresher course at my computer that afternoon on the biochemistry of the immune response. In these diseases, the body's own defense mechanisms are activated as usual but fail to switch off, causing the normally helpful mast cells to release an excess of cytokines, which leads to destruction of the blood vessels. That's why the injured blood vessels leak plasma in the early stages of vasculitis. As the damage becomes more severe, the blood cells spill out as well. Our mystery fluid was explained.

My cell phone rang as I was immersed in my research. It was my doctor's name on the caller ID. In the adrenaline rush of dealing with two odd emergencies, I had forgotten I was a cancer patient waiting for the phone call that might set me free.

"Hi, this is Julie from Dr. M's office," the caller said. My heart fell when she said she wasn't calling about my scans. "Dr. M wanted me to call you to let you know that your white blood cell count came back at a 'panic' low, 1.2. He wants you to stay away from people and animals."

No doubt it wasn't good to have a white blood cell count at a "panic" value when working on dogs with circovirus. "I'll see what I can do," I said and went back to my patients.

Almost immediately my phone rang again. This time it was my former associate, Dr. Stacy, who had retired after having two babies. "I hear you have a very sick black Lab there," she said.

"Actually, we have two very sick black Labs here. How did you know?"

"Wrigly's owner is my neighbor. What do you think it is?"

"There's something really bad going on with these two." I told her the details of the cases and what the state veterinarian had said. "They think it's this circovirus."

I explained that nearly all the other dogs with this disease in Cincy had died, so I wanted to get these dogs to the emergency clinic for overnight care. We were closing in an hour. These two dogs were too sick to go home and too big to spend the night in my whirlpool tub. They either would have to go to the emergency clinic or spend the night at Elm Ridge unattended.

Stacy told me that her husband, Mike, was on duty at the emergency clinic that night, so she would get Wrigly there. Now, I needed to get Bella to transfer to the emergency clinic. Unfortunately, Bella's owner did not have the financial resources for overnight care at the ER. She opted to keep Bella with us overnight. I would keep an eye on Bella through a webcam, and she would get fluids through an IV pump. The situation was less than ideal. I explained that if Bella worsened during the night, we would not be able to do anything until morning.

"You've done everything you can," her owner said. "It's going to be up to God. All we can do is pray."

I headed home that night in a bit of a daze. The chemo demons, which I had been able to ignore through the afternoon, resumed their beat down.

Steve had prepared a special meal, a salad we had enjoyed at an Italian restaurant in Oregon. He was proud of himself for mimicking the recipe of spring greens, chopped pears, pistachios, strawberries, and dried cherries doused in champagne vinaigrette and topped with roasted asparagus and a perfectly fried sunny-side-up egg. Eating food at this stage of chemo was like chewing on gasoline-soaked newspaper. I did my best, but I knew most of my serving would go to Dillie.

Just as we were beginning to talk about the intense day I had had, I received a call from Mike at the emergency clinic. Soon after Wrigly arrived, he started to develop neurologic signs, seizured, and then passed away. The owners had allowed a postmortem. Mike had found blood-tinged fluid in Wrigly's abdomen and chest, and hemorrhages everywhere. Just what had happened to the Cincy dogs.

"They need samples of everything," I told Mike. "We've got blood and stool going to them already. If you drop off specimens, we'll send them, too."

He promised he would drop them off the next day.

"You barely touched your salad," Steve said, as we cleared the dishes.

I hated to see Steve so disappointed. He shooed me out of the kitchen and up to bed. As I climbed the stairs, I felt so grateful to my husband. My cancer had been his battle, too.

I headed to the office an hour early the next morning, my fifty-third birthday. I was still whipped despite a restful night. Chemo fatigue could not be washed away with sleep. It was Saturday, so I had only a half day ahead of me, and then I could crash.

I found Bella alive, but no better. The mystery fluid still oozed from her gums and she remained profoundly weak. Her breathing had not improved, though it hadn't worsened, either.

I sat down to read a number of articles about how viruses like Ebola used the body's immune system to kill the afflicted and began to understand what was happening to these dogs. It occurred to me that I shouldn't just be treating this as an infection, but like an anaphylaxis, a severe allergic reaction. The biochemistry was similar. A person having a fatal reaction to a bee sting died not from the bee but from the chemicals released by his own immune system.

I hesitated to reach for corticosteroids and antihistamines. In human medicine, corticosteroids have been largely replaced by other drugs used to prevent the "cytokine storm." These drugs cost tens of thousands of dollars per dose. In the veterinary world, cortisone and antihistamines were my only options.

I didn't know if this approach would work for Bella or if it would hurt her. Steroid use in a case like hers was very controversial. If her illness was a rampant bacterial infection, the immune suppression produced by the steroid would make it harder for her body to kill the bacteria. I was already blasting her with two very powerful intravenous antibiotics, so that base was covered. Her own immune system was killing her, not the agent that triggered it.

I decided to give it a try. Bella might not be knocking on death's door just yet, but she was definitely on his front porch.

She didn't even open her eyes as I lifted her leg to access her IV. Despite an entire day of fluids and antibiotics, she was no stronger or brighter than she had been when she came to the clinic. Other than the mystery fluid, I had learned that one of the distinctive signs of this disease was extreme weakness. I had seen dogs this weak before, but only many days after taking ill. Only dogs with a toxin, anaphylaxis, abrupt blood loss, torsions, or trauma were wiped out so suddenly. The hundreds of septic shock cases I had seen in the past had taken days before they had gotten this bad. Bella and Wrigly had been sick for less than twelve hours when they came in, and the Cincinnati dogs died less than eight hours from the time they got sick. Whatever this crazy bug was, it was the most frighteningly aggressive agent in dogs I had ever seen.

I gave Bella a low dose of an intravenous, fast-acting steroid.

In less than two hours, Bella was a completely different dog. The steroids were working their magic. Her temperature returned to normal. The nasty oozing finally stopped. Her breathing was normal. She stood up for the first time since we had admitted her. She barked at us when we checked on her. She drank water. She wagged her tail! Seeing that tail wag was the best birthday gift ever. "Good job, Bella!" I said. "You go, girl!"

By one p.m., the end of my half day, Bella was starting to eat. She was well enough to go home, with the stipulation that the owner would meet me back at the clinic on Sunday and Monday.

The Sunday checkup was encouraging. Bella was a little fatigued, but she was eating and had normal respirations and heart rate. Her will to live was strong, and so was mine, despite ten rounds of chemo and panicking white blood cells.

Before going home, I thought it would be a good idea to post a warning about circovirus on the clinic's Facebook page. I wanted to warn people that if their dog became mysteriously ill to get the sick pet to their veterinarian immediately. I described our cases and wrote an account of the Cincinnati dogs. My post set off an Internet firestorm. People shared the post with hundreds of others, who shared the warning with hundreds more. Somewhere along the line, reporters read the post and quoted me. When I got to the office on Monday morning, all I wanted was to hear from my oncologist. Instead, my answering machine was full of messages from people across the country describing the symptoms of their sick dogs. My e-mail in-box contained hundreds of similar messages, many with photos of their sick dogs. Then the reporters started calling.

At the end of the day, just as I grabbed my car keys, my cell phone buzzed. A veterinarian from Cleveland introduced himself and said he had gotten my number from the state vet. He had a patient much like Bella who was acutely sick, with fluid oozing from her gums. He asked how I had treated Bella.

I explained about the low dose of steroid I had tried that

caused Bella to have a remarkable turnaround. "She went from dying to eating in just hours," I said. "Controlling the immune response seems to be the key."

As soon as I ended the call, my phone buzzed again. The caller was one of my professors from Ohio State, a brilliant pathologist and an exacting scientist, from whom I had not heard since graduation. I was surprised to learn that he had spent years researching the circovirus and had been watching our case. He commended me on my success.

"I didn't do anything," I protested. "I never even heard of this virus before this week."

"No, no," he said. "You've done a good job."

He asked about my illness, and I told him I was waiting for news.

"It's going to be good news," he said with confidence. "You're going to be fine, because you've got more work to do."

I believed him.

With that, I put my phone on vibrate and headed home.

Steve was waiting for me with Dillie when I pulled up to the garage. My phone started vibrating as I got out of the car.

"No more calls," Steve said. "You need to give yourself a break."

I glanced at the caller ID. It was my oncologist. This time it had to be my scan results. I waved Steve off and answered.

"The scans are clear," he reported.

I wanted to fall on my knees. Chemo was done. He told me he would repeat scans every three months, but for now, I was in remission. For whatever time I had until the next time, I had my life back.

Chapter 36

~~~~~~

A New Lease on Life

As spring turned to summer, the pain of losing our beloved Lady lessened, and we could remember her with smiles instead of tears. I was still recovering from the chemo.

I knew that a big part of my recovery was fueled by the support of Dillie's fans. As they became aware of my illness, they showered me with prayers and love. Though I only knew these people through our connection with Dillie, their kindness surprised me. I could not fail with all this love supporting my spirit.

Even with the good news, I was secretly afraid, because I didn't know what came next. And then I found the answer—I just had to live.

I hadn't told anyone about my fears. I had been preparing to die for nine months. I had bought extra life insurance, made a will, made arrangements for the potential succession of my corporation, and prearranged my funeral. Every night during that time, I wrote a note to Steve recalling a special moment in our life together so that after I was gone he could relive our love. I had gotten my affairs in order, just as the surgeon had told me to. I was all set to die. The only thing I had not prepared for was living.

I had to begin by celebrating with Lady, even if she was only there in spirit. She had been through it all with me, right up until the day she could no longer walk.

"We did it, girl," I said to her grave. I imagined her tail wagging.

We had told Dillie's webcam viewers that we would communicate the scan results with a signal. If Dillie was wearing my bright blue chemo headscarf, they would know the news was good. That night at her usual eight o'clock snack time, Dillie wore the scarf around her neck. Her viewers cheered from our hometown all the way to Perth, Australia. I was grateful beyond measure to have this extraordinary crowd in my corner.

Steve and I decided to take a trip to celebrate my new lease on life. When my treatment began, I set a goal for myself. I focused on taking a blues cruise when I finished chemo and was in remission. While Zeh watched Dillie and Spazz, we went down to Florida to take that cruise, which I called the mojito tour, with my friend Mae, my housemate in vet school.

Mae and I had joined a group of students on a trip to

the Keys on spring break during our second year of school. We were supposed to stay at Bahia Honda State Park, but about forty miles short of our destination on Grassy Key, we were too tired to go on. Instead of keeping to our plans, we turned in to the first campground we saw, the Jolly Roger.

Back then, the Keys were full of cheesy trailer parks, motels, and campgrounds that catered to locals and budget-restricted visitors like us. The Jolly Roger was one of the worst, but our stopping in there wound up being one of the most important decisions in Mae's life. During our stay at the Jolly Roger, Mae met and fell instantly in love with her future husband, Mark.

A few years later, I visited Mae and Mark, who still lived at the Jolly Roger. I was sitting in their trailer reading one day, waiting for them to come back from the store, when their screen door popped open and in walked a stranger. He didn't notice me and made for the fridge. He grabbed a beer and turned to leave, then saw me.

"Oh, hi," he said, embarrassed. "I'm Nander. I live next door."

"Hi, I'm Mae's friend, Melanie."

The stranger was tall and muscular, with an overgrown mop of brown hair and a long, scraggly beard. He was a concrete finisher by trade, a tough but lucrative job in an area like the Keys, where all-concrete homes were sprouting faster than mangroves.

He stayed and asked me about my work, my life, and the book I was reading. At the time, I was enjoying Carl Hiaasen's *Tourist Season* immensely. Nander asked if he could read it when I was finished. By the time Mae and

Mark came back with the groceries, Nander and I were chatting like old friends. Mark carried in a case of Old Milwaukee.

Nander greeted him by waving the beer he had taken from the fridge and saying, "Good thinking. You were out of beer."

Later that night, Nander joined us for dinner. Mark was a crab and lobster fisherman and had brought back a huge pile of stone crab claws from his boat. The four of us sat at Mark's picnic table and hammered open crab claws for hours.

I didn't see Nander again before I left. Two years later, I visited my friends again, and this time, I stayed at the motel next to the Jolly Roger instead of in their trailer. As I arrived and unpacked, there was a knock at the door. Standing in the doorway was Nander, with a rose in his hand. He had shaved his burly beard. Since I had never fully seen his handsome face before, I barely recognized him.

"It's me!" he said. "Nander. Don't you remember me?"

Of course I did, mostly because Mae had been teasing me about him since my last visit.

Nander joined us for dinner every night that week. Afterward, he and I would walk out to the pier and look at the stars and talk. On my last night there, he didn't appear, and his trailer, which was next to Mark's and Mae's, stayed dark.

People in the Keys have a way of coming and going and sometimes disappearing completely. I knew I might never see Nander again, but I wanted to thank him for the times we had shared that week. I told Mae I would write him a note and leave it on his trailer door.

"What's his real name?" I asked Mae.

She shrugged. "Everyone just calls him 'Nander,'" she said. "Because the day he moved in here, he looked like a caveman, a Neanderthal."

"Steve," Mark said. "Steve Heathman."

A day after my return to Ohio, the mystery of Nander's disappearance was solved. He called me to apologize and to explain.

He and a friend Gary, whose Keys name was Gagoo, had rented a boat to fish for grouper that day. Starting out on the bay side of the Seven Mile Bridge, they fished here and there catching yellowfin snapper, but no grouper. They decided they would motor farther down toward Key West where Steve knew a grouper spot, a deep area surrounded by abandoned lobster traps.

They had packed all the necessities: rods, reels, nets, chum, bait, and a cooler full of ice and beer. The one thing they had forgotten was a compass. After buzzing along for hours, they realized something was wrong. They could no longer see land, and Key West should have come into view an hour earlier. The cloudless sky and turquoise water gave them no indication where they were.

Just when they realized they were lost, they saw land ahead. They docked at a small wooden pier where a man and his son where fishing with poles and bobbers.

Steve asked the man, "Is this Key West?"

"Como?" the Hispanic man answered.

"Cayo Hueso," Steve said. "Is this *Cayo Hueso*?"

"No, no," the man said, looking at Steve as though he was from Mars. *"Es Flamingo."*

"Flamingo!" Steve said. "It can't be! Flamingo is in the

Everglades!" He looked around and saw the familiar vegetation and landscape of the glades.

They had motored for three hours in the wrong direction.

"It was a good thing we were bay side," Steve told me on the phone, "or the Cuban we met at the dock would have been a real Cuban!"

Life is so funny. Sometimes it is best to not have a compass, to not follow a plan. Mae met Mark, and I met Steve, all thanks to a chance turn into the Jolly Roger trailer park. Now, some twenty-five years later, we were all coming together again to celebrate on a blues cruise.

Mae and I enjoyed virgin mojitos at sunset on the pool deck the first night, while Cajun blues master Tab Benoit played. I had pushed myself through the darkest days of my treatment to get to this point, and I savored the moment. My drink contained no alcohol, but I had never felt more intoxicated.

Chapter 37

~~~~~~~~

Dillie, Meet Willie

When we returned to Ohio, Dillie seemed lonely. Steve tried to spend extra time with her whenever he could, and Spazz demanded that she groom him often. She seemed forlorn up on her bed without Lady. A year after Lady's death, I told Steve we should think about getting another dog, one that looked like Lady so Dillie would not be afraid. I didn't think Dillie would mistake the new dog for Lady. I believed that Dillie would associate the dog with her friend.

Steve wanted a bloodhound, but I was adamant about getting a poodle. When one of Dillie's fans e-mailed me a photo of a black standard poodle who needed a new home, I knew I was going to win the battle. A little smaller than Lady, she looked bright and elegant in the photos. Her name was Willie, which I took as a sign that she would be the perfect companion for Dillie.

I asked Steve to leave Dillie outside for a while one morning. I had arranged for the breeder to bring Willie over for a trial meeting with Dillie. When the van pulled up the drive, Steve was cleaning the pool and Dillie was right behind him. As soon as Willie bounded out of the van, Steve took one look and knew that we had our new dog.

Dillie seemed to accept Willie immediately, licking and kissing her just as she had with Lady. Willie showed only curiosity, not fear or aggression, toward her new friend.

There was still a brief adjustment period. Willie spent the first day staring out the windows, looking down the driveway, waiting for her old owner to return. When we went to bed that night, Willie stood on her hind feet and stared longingly out the upstairs window. The sun had not completely set, and after surveying the drive and front yard, she began growling.

I got up and looked out the window. "What are you seeing, Willie?"

A small herd of does was crossing our yard. Willie was growling at deer, the same species she had played with all day. On alert, Dillie came into the room as I climbed back into bed. She licked Willie while the dog stood at the window, growling at Dillie's wild cousins.

By the next day, Willie had settled into our family. She raced around the yard, leaping logs like a champion horse and rolling in the grass. I tossed her a new toy, a stuffed sock monkey, and she ran away, squeaking the monkey, to lie under a flowering crabapple tree.

Dillie followed her around the yard, fascinated by her hair ribbons and soft curly fur. Spazz plodded along a few steps behind, anxious to be part of the group.

I was happy that our little family felt complete again.

Chapter 38

Hoofstock

Dillie's fans took Willie into their hearts. They were thrilled by Dillie's new sister and sent boxes of toys and treats. The kindness of Dillie's extended family, from just about everywhere on Earth, kept Steve and me in awe.

"Let's plan a big party and invite all her fans," Steve said. "A big backyard barbecue and swim party. We need to thank them for all the cards and gifts."

I loved the idea. I had been thinking about meeting Dillie's fans for a while, especially the ones who had been praying for me and helping me through the rough times.

I also knew that my cancer was back. I recognized immediately the telltale pain in my lower right belly. Soon I would be back in chemo and would return to the limbo of life as a cancer patient, unable to make any plans or goals other than just to get through another week, day, hour. I was eager to meet these wonderful people who had become so much a part of our life.

We put out the word and invited Dillie's fans to a party we called "Hoofstock." More than 150 Dillie fans, whom we had never met but communicated with daily, poured into the yard on a perfect, unseasonably warm day in early September. They came from as far away as Chicago and caused a minor traffic jam on our remote country road.

Dillie was the perfect hostess. She did not tire of meeting anyone, especially the many who brought her roses, carnations, and candy. She stayed outside most of the afternoon, retreating to her bed only at the end of the day. Even then, she welcomed visitors in her room, with an elegance that would have made Neffie proud.

Willie was also excited to meet so many people. Instead of bringing visitors toys as Lady had, Willie stood on her hind legs and hugged newcomers with her forelegs. She ran from person to person wagging her tail and stood up to bestow Willie hugs.

Steve and I caught her sneaking over to the fire pit to steal hot dogs and burgers left warming over a low fire. With shameless aplomb, she tested the various edges of the pit to see which entry point was coolest. Eventually, to prevent Willie from devouring the entire buffet, we had to assign one of Steve's buddies to guard the grill.

We were amazed by how many people came out to see Dillie. At nine p.m., just as the last guest was heading down the driveway, a Dillie fan called us on the phone. "Are we too late?" she asked. "We drove all the way from Chicago, and it took longer than we thought it would."

We couldn't disappoint fans who had driven that far just to see Dillie, but we were ready to crawl into bed. We arranged a hotel for them and planned a private Dillie visit for the next day.

Chapter 39

Every Life Is a Gift

As we went to bed that night, the entire menagerie camped out in our room. I was glad that Steve didn't yet know what was ahead. He would find out soon enough— the CT scans were scheduled for the following week. Tonight, he could sleep blissfully.

I wasn't scared, though. This time I was grateful. I was grateful for the entire cast of characters and improbable events that Dillie's life had brought to mine.

I always wondered why Mr. Glick, the deer farmer, had brought her to me in the first place. I asked him about it once, and he had no explanation. What had been so special about the dying fawn that made him take extraordinary measures to save her? When I slipped the IV into her jugular vein, I set off a chain reaction that affected the rest of my life.

Would it have mattered if Dillie had died on the farm? The universe would not have skipped a beat, but the Creator had other plans for this abandoned deer and for me.

Though Dillie cannot leave our five-acre property, she has touched people around the world. Her reach is a miracle of modern communications, but it is also a miracle of love. This blind rescued deer has had an impact that continues to ripple throughout the world. I felt confident that my life had purpose and meaning and would have a lasting effect.

Love and providence are the foundations of Dillie's life. As I marveled at all that had come to me because of Dillie, I began to see that in saving her life, I had saved my own. It was a revelation that gave me the sense that my path was not yet at an end. I was no longer afraid to stare into the unknown.

As Dillie jumped on the bed to snuggle, I knew I could leave fear and regret behind and continue my journey with gratitude and joy.

Epilogue

New Year's Day, 2015

As I write this in my little upstairs office, Dillie is right next to me, licking my hand and tipping over my cup of tea. I am listening to Christmas music and Dillie is making a pest of herself as she explores the room. Willie is sleeping on the sofa behind me, grumbling each time Dillie gets too close. Dillie just shut the door with her nose, so now she is trapped in here with me. Eventually, she will get tired of knocking over my chai and will lie down and listen to the music.

I am fighting cancer again, but with confidence this time. No matter what the disease does to me, it cannot erase the impact of my life. It cannot reverse the work I have done, or end the friendships I have made, or unwrite this book. It cannot end the love I share with my husband. It cannot erase the smiles I have seen on children's faces when they meet Dillie. It cannot remove the cherished memories I have of all the wonderful Dillie fans who reach out to us from around the world, sending us love and prayers.

I will continue on my journey without fear, with the peace of knowing that my path is lit by love, joy, and a deer named Dillie.

My love and gratitude go out to all you wonderful animal people out there. Thank you for opening your hearts to us and to all the animals in your life. You know the rewards of being an animal person outweigh the pristine carpets and undamaged furniture you have sacrificed. Be like your pets and live with all the joy you can. Every life has meaning and is a celebration of God, whatever you perceive Him to be. If a little spotted fawn with no reason to live can bring love to people a world away, then the love each of us gives and the life each of us lives leaves a mark on the universe.

All of us animal people know the most important lesson of all: Love endures forever.

With love,

Melanie Butera, DVM

Acknowledgments

To the thousands of Dillie fans who have written, visited, or watched Dillie but whom I could not mention specifically in the book, thank you so much for sharing your love with us.

I am so grateful to my family, friends, colleagues, and co-workers who have supported me in good times and in bad.

I owe so much to my staff at the Stark County Veterinary Emergency Clinic and the Elm Ridge Animal Hospital. Eric Lafreniere, Angie Shultz-Martin, Shawna Koch-Pitts, Rhonda Stinard, Joelle Fellows, Noel Meszaros, Jessica Covell, Ashlee Witmer, Curtis Bohannon, Dr. Stacy Bridges, Dr. Mike Bridges, Amy Justice, Sherry Todd, Alicin Golliher, Sally Westbrooks—you are top professionals with big hearts. You have made doing my job more of a pleasure.

A special thank you to Mark Zinni, who started it all.

I thank David Vigliano, my agent, and his associate, Thomas Flannery Jr., for discovering my self-published book and encouraging me to seek a broader audience. Not only did they put me together with Diane Reverand, who worked with me to create a new manuscript from the old, but they also found me Regan Arts, the best possible publisher for this book.

A million thank-yous to Diane Reverand, whose passion, skill, and enthusiasm brought this project to life and to Daniel E. Slotnik, who assisted her in getting the manuscript into shape.

The extraordinary team at Regan Arts saw the potential in Dillie's story and, more important, fell in love with Dillie and the rest of our crazy family. My editor, Alexis Gargagliano, was passionate about my book from the start. Her work resulted in a much more powerfully told story. So many people were involved in making *Dillie the Deer* at Regan Arts: Richard Ljoenes, the creative director, Lynne Ciccaglione, the managing editor, Mia Abrahams, George Bick, the sales director and early champion, and Judith Regan, whose savvy and vision have made her such a legendary publisher. I am honored that you chose to take on the story of an abandoned fawn who has brought so much to my life and to the lives of many others.

I have to include the incredible oncology team at Akron General Hospital in my thanks, as well as Mary Ann Williamson and Tim Quinn, cancer survivor and warrior, who has been such an inspiration to me along with all the "survivor strong" cancer patients out there.

About the Author

Melanie R. Butera, DVM, is a veterinarian with more than twenty years of emergency experience. She has owned the Elm Ridge Animal Hospital for the past ten years and the Stark County Veterinary Emergency Clinic before that. She has treated more than 100,000 emergency cases in her career and now enjoys the different challenges of private practice work. Dr. Butera and her husband, Steve Heathman, live in Canal Fulton, Ohio.

CONTACT INFORMATION

Dillie's website: www.dilliedeer.com

Address: 464-A Etheridge Blvd. S.
         Canal Fulton, Ohio 44614

E-mail: dilliethedeer@live.com